"God has given Aaron a really unique platform to love on people, and he is having a huge impact for the kingdom of God around the world. *Outrageous* is a collection of hilarious, faith-filled stories he has collected on the journey. I really believe it will inspire you to embrace the abundant life God has for you, and it will challenge you to use whatever gifts and opportunities he gives you to be his hands and feet."

Todd Mullins, senior pastor of Christ Fellowship

"*Outrageous: Awake to the Unexpected Adventures of Everyday Faith* by Aaron Tredway is just that, an adventure of faith! So often our faith is anything but an adventure. Through the pages of this book, get ready to be awakened to the great adventure of living on mission with Jesus!"

Derwin L. Gray, lead pastor of Transformation Church; author of *Limitless Life*

"Some speakers inspire. Some writers inspire. Few can switch-hit with the same results. Aaron Tredway can and *does* in these amazing races—twenty-four chapters of outrageous adventures around the world. Honest—I read half of these page-turning stories to my wife and we both agreed—*Outrageous* is the perfect book for family, friends, colleagues, and clients. *Whew!* The stories are incredible, like 'Sleep in the Middle,' or 'Son of the King,' or 'Jesus Calling' (my favorite). Aaron's heart for God and every soul on the planet shines through. *Outrageous* touched my heart."

John Pearson, author of *Mastering the Management Buckets*

"*Outrageous* is a very entertaining, exciting, and encouraging read on the phenomenal things that can and will happen when we are willing to let go of fear and doubt and boldly go where God leads us. After reading Aaron's book, I am ~~~~~~~~ onvinced that a Christ-centered ! ~~~~~~~~~~~~~~~~ e more abundantly. If you have doubts that God can make the impossible possible, read *Outrageous: Awake to the Unexpected Adventures of Everyday Faith*, because Aaron Tredway's life will make you reconsider!"

Jerod Cherry, three-time Super Bowl champion; cohost of *The Really Big Show* on ESPN Cleveland

"This book ends with a simple but profound question, 'What do you have to lose?' I had been a Christian since I was twelve but did not become a Christ-follower until I was forty. Everything, *everything* changed . . . life became fuller, not easy . . . became joyful even in hardship . . . became content but not necessarily comfortable . . . became *peaceful* even in the midst of uncertainty. My life began an *Outrageous* journey and that is the only way to experience *real* life. All the important relationships in my life have exploded to a deeper level of love and commitment—my wife, my children, my friends. I even began to love my enemies. Why? Because I began to see the clear message and journey that Aaron so vividly describes in *Outrageous*. This culture promotes the prosperity of comfort, chasing after riches, and entitlement. But Jesus says 'whoever wishes to save his life will *lose* it, but whoever *loses* his life for my sake will *find* it. For what will it profit a man if he gains the whole world and forfeits his soul?' *Outrageous* is a must-read because you will ask yourself *the* question, 'What do you have to lose?' . . . and in the process you might find life, and life more than abundant!"

Dr. Jeff Duke, creator and author of 3 Dimensional Coaching

"Aaron Tredway, in his book *Outrageous*, takes us with him on a wild adventure and an exhilarating ride involving people, sports, culture, and spirituality. Aaron is one who knows how God takes ordinary people like us and allows us to experience life like we could never have imagined! You'll love *Outrageous*."

Dave Gibbons, founder of Xealots.org; author of *Xealots: Defying the Gravity of Normality*

OUTRAGEOUS

AWAKE TO THE
UNEXPECTED ADVENTURES
OF EVERYDAY FAITH

AARON TREDWAY

BakerBooks

a division of Baker Publishing Group
Grand Rapids, Michigan

Published by Baker Books
a division of Baker Publishing Group
P.O. Box 6287, Grand Rapids, MI 49516-6287
www.bakerbooks.com

Printed in the United States of America

Library of Congress Cataloging-in-Publication Data
Names: Tredway, Aaron, 1976– author.
Title: Outrageous : awake to the unexpected adventures of everyday faith / Aaron
    Tredway.
Description: Grand Rapids : Baker Books, 2016.
Identifiers: LCCN 2016020333 | ISBN 9780801019296 (pbk.)
Subjects: LCSH: Christian life.
Classification: LCC BV4501.3 .T726 2016 | DDC 248.4—dc23
LC record available at https://lccn.loc.gov/2016020333

Some names and details have been changed to protect the privacy of the individuals involved.

Published in association with the literary agent Tawny Johnson of D. C. Jacobson & Associates LLC, an Author Management Company, www.dcjacobson.com.

16 17 18 19 20 21 22   7 6 5 4 3 2 1

To Noah:
you are outrageous.

CONTENTS

CONTENTS

INTRODUCTION

Waking Up

I USED TO HAVE A FRIEND NAMED HARRY. Harry was one of those guys who had all the stuff. Not like David Beckham has great hair or Taylor Swift writes cool pop songs, but Harry had what *he* needed. I met Harry working out in the gym; he was on a recumbent bike, I was on an elliptical. Actually, we were at the gym and I was working out. Harry was not.

The day I met Harry I had just moved from Cape Town, South Africa, to Cleveland, Ohio—in *January*. Don't judge me. I spent the first twenty-two years of my life in California, but almost every year since has been a total free-for-all. I realize moving to Cleveland in January seems outrageous, but so was sleeping between a four-hundred-pound Zimbabwean couple in their mud hut, being mistaken for the son of a king, dancing naked around a bonfire at three a.m. with a pygmy village chief, or the time I spent living in a yurt, burning cow dung for warmth, somewhere in Outer Mongolia. I've noticed that outrageous things often happen in my life when I'm awake to their possibility and willing to act when the opportunity arises. Needless to say, an outrageous life is my ambition, and the stories I share in this book are all about the outrageous things that happen when you invite God to navigate the course of your life and open yourself to opportunities you might not have ever considered.

Harry was a little outrageous as well. The first time I saw him in the gym he was dressed from head to toe in the latest, most fashionable, high-tech workout gear you can buy. Some might think Harry had gone a bit overboard while shopping at the local sporting goods store. He had Dri-FIT everything: shirt, shorts, windbreaker, wristbands—you name it, Harry had it. I suppose I didn't check his underpants, but we had only just met.

Harry intrigued me, and not just because of his gear. At the time of our meeting Harry was at least eighty-five years old. Trust me, that's a conservative guess—he could have easily passed for one hundred and five. A thick yellow headband complete with the iconic swoosh was plastered to his forehead, holding back the caged yet ferocious white lion that was his static-filled afro.

Harry wasn't the fastest moving guy in the gym, but at least he was there. Actually, Harry wore an expensive GPS watch that complemented the color scheme of his outfit, and as I've thought about that watch, I'm convinced it was a family tracking device. I'm guessing the family told Harry it would track his workout, but I'm sure they used it to keep track of him.

Harry cycled at about five revolutions per minute. That's probably just faster than a baby worm can crawl. He maintained this clip for some time, but then without warning he stopped. He didn't stop to get a drink, wipe the perspiration from his brow, or check his Twitter feed. He just stopped. Then his head slumped over. Then his body began to sink down on the bike.

Before we go on, let me pose a question. If you saw an eighty-something person with his or her eyes closed slumped over like a burlap sack of potatoes hanging over a barstool, sitting motionless in the gym—or anywhere for that matter—*what would you think?*

Fearing the worst, I stepped off my elliptical and slowly walked toward Harry. It was a very slow walk. I'm not sure what I feared more, confirming Harry had in fact taken his last bike ride or having to perform mouth-to-mouth resuscitation. I'm being serious. I went to high school in an era when the most famous people on television hung out on Malibu Beach wearing red Speedos all day. That was the only motivation I needed to sign up for first aid training to become a lifeguard. I owned the Speedo. I was certified. The issue was that Harry did not fit my longstanding vision of whom I might need to resuscitate.

Now standing directly over Harry, I attempted to check his breathing but he was likely receiving a low-grade radio frequency from Thailand, based on the size and volume of his headphones. I put my hand on his arm. He didn't move. I jostled his boney shoulder a bit, still no response. With very little to lose, I pulled the right headphone away from his ear and managed to wedge my head in between. I had read a few stories about Jesus calling dead people to life, so I figured it was worth a shot. After all, Lazarus had been dead for days when Jesus found him; Harry had only been dancing on the streets of gold for a matter of minutes.

I yelled, "Wake up!"

And he did!

As Harry opened his eyes and slowly surveyed his surroundings, he looked like a newborn baby discovering life for the very first time. Not wanting to startle him any more than I already had, I quickly said, "Sir, are you ok?" He closed his eyes and began shaking his head, as if to say, *No, no, I'm not.*

Still shaking his head, Harry asked, "Where am I?"

I wanted to express my relief that he was still in the land of the living. I refrained. Instead I very gently said, "You are in the gym, sir."

He began shaking his head again. Clearly frustrated, Harry said, "I'm supposed to be working out." I decided it was a rhetorical statement so I just kept listening. "My grandkids gave me all this stuff to wear and they told me I need to work out three days each week, but every time I come to the gym, I fall asleep!"

That was the beginning of my friendship with Harry. For the next few years I would see Harry on Monday, Wednesday, and Friday most weeks. We usually spoke, but not for long, because Harry was always too busy sleeping.

A few years into my friendship with Harry, he missed a Monday at the gym. He never missed a Monday. But then he missed Wednesday. He missed Friday as well. Just as Harry had abruptly stopped peddling his bike the first day we met, one day Harry just stopped coming to the gym altogether. For weeks I'd routinely glance toward his bike during my workout, hoping that Harry would return. He never did.

The thing about Harry is that he would come to the gym every Monday, Wednesday, and Friday intending to work out, but he was literally asleep on the job. I think he was figuratively asleep as well, not actively using the stuff he had received from his grandkids for the purpose for which it was given to him. I've noticed sometimes I live my life like that—*asleep*.

When you are asleep, you might be present but you're not usually active. Sleep is a passive state of existence. You are unaware of the things happening around you and stuck in a cycle of monotony. When you are asleep you accept the rhythm of routine and you don't seek change.

On the other hand, when you are awake you are aware of things happening around you. You are alert to danger but also opportunity. You are cognizant of your surroundings and attentive to varying situations. People who are awake are ready to seize an opportunity when it presents itself, often taking risks that would otherwise be considered inopportune if you weren't conscious of a potentially unforeseen outcome.

Over the years I interacted with Harry, he taught me the value of being awake, especially when you've been given everything you need to accomplish whatever it is that God wants you to do.

I confess. I drive a Nissan. I eat oatmeal for breakfast. I mow my own lawn. Every Thursday I take the garbage out to the trashcan and the trashcan out to the curb for collection. I wash dishes and cars and clothes and floors, and sometimes pets and babies. I pump my own gas. I stand in line at the grocery store. I even clean the toilet.

But despite the routine that often characterizes my everyday experience, I'm still convinced that the life of faith is supposed to be something more.

I think that's what Jesus was about. He wanted people to experience *more* than our everyday life can offer. Jesus had a name for the type of life he wants for people—*abundant*. I like to think of the life Jesus offers as *outrageous*. I know, *outrageous* is a pretty, well, outrageous word, but I think it describes the abundant life Jesus often spoke of.

Something outrageous is unconventional, extravagant, or remarkable; it surpasses all reasonable bounds. Sure, my life doesn't always feel extravagant or remarkable, but maybe it should. Maybe if we were a little more awake to the opportunities, events, and adventures Jesus wants for us, our life would look and feel different. Maybe we were created to live an outrageous life, even though our everyday experiences might not always seem entirely outrageous in the moment.

I've noticed that Jesus seemed to define an outrageous life by different standards than most of us do. Those who knew them best described many of his first followers as "unschooled, ordinary men" (see Acts 4:13), but when they decided to follow Jesus, his first followers seemed to leave the *ordinary* behind. The book of Acts alone is filled with stories of these seemingly ordinary people doing outrageous, extraordinary things. For example, the apostle Peter was an average fisherman, but when he connected his life to Jesus, *outrageous* is the only way to describe the things that began to happen.

In the New Testament, Acts 3 records a story about a man named Peter and his friend John, who were walking into a church at three o'clock in the afternoon when they saw a man who was unable to walk from birth. The man was sitting in front of the church, begging, as he always did. So when the man saw Peter and John, of course, he asked them for money. But money is not what Peter gave him; instead he looked directly at the man and said, "In the name of Jesus, walk!" And the man immediately jumped to his feet for the first time in his entire life, and he walked. I think that's *outrageous*.

Peter did plenty of other outrageous things too, like the time he raised a woman from death to life, or another time when he was being held in a maximum-security prison for proclaiming his faith and God enabled him to walk out the front door despite the guards and everything designed to keep him inside.

The Bible records countless stories of Jesus giving his followers the ability to heal sick people, resurrect dead people, and travel the world doing things that most of us would never imagine were possible. Ultimately, the original followers of Jesus, though they were thought to be unschooled, ordinary men, started a movement of people called out of their ordinary circumstances to form a group we now call the church, and two thousand years later this group continues to thrive and influence every corner of the universe. Apparently ordinary people can do extraordinary things and live outrageous lives, if they so choose.

The lives of those who followed Jesus in the Bible were filled with unexpected opportunity, possibility, potential, and adventure. These people came from different backgrounds, countries, and professions. They all had different cultural practices and traditions. They looked outwardly similar to their friends and neighbors. But they were different. They might have appeared to be ordinary, but when they connected their lives to Jesus, outrageous things began to happen.

Several years ago I decided I wanted God to do outrageous things through my life too. Not because I'm an outrageous person but because I have an outrageous God who can do outrageous things and has offered an outrageous life to anyone who wants it. You and I get to choose.

This book chronicles some outrageous opportunities, events, and adventures that I have participated in because of my faith in Jesus. I am absolutely certain that there is nothing extraordinary about my faith, but I know an extraordinary God. The thing is, I don't believe you need extraordinary faith to experience an outrageous life. Gospel writers Matthew and Luke both record

Jesus telling his closest friends that if they had even the smallest amount of faith they could move mountains and all sorts of other impossibilities. It seems to me that even small amounts of faith in Jesus, exercised amid ordinary circumstances, have the potential to create outrageous outcomes.

I think that was Jesus's point to his friends, and to us as well—a small amount of faith, let's call it *everyday faith*, has the power to move us into opportunities, events, and even adventures that we might not have ever thought possible.

This book is all about waking up to the outrageous potential and opportunities made available to anyone who has faith in Jesus. We might not be able to move mountains ourselves, but Jesus is more than able. I hope the stories in this book entertain you but even more that they inspire you to be awake to the outrageous things that are possible through everyday faith in an extraordinary God.

Jesus talked about how faith can move mountains, but maybe *what* you move isn't as important as your willingness *to* move, and your belief that Jesus is able to take your ordinary life and use it to accomplish extraordinary things.

Now, I don't know about you, but that's what I want—an *outrageous* life. So, I suppose the question is, are you *awake*?

1

I'M IN

I GREW UP IN CALIFORNIA. When I was five years old my dad signed me up to play soccer. He may have regretted that decision. Prior to signing me up, I don't think my dad had actually ever seen soccer—I know he had never played. But in California, kids can begin playing organized team sports at age five and soccer season happens to come before baseball season. He's never told me directly, but I'm pretty sure my dad thought I would be a better baseball player if I played soccer. I've never played one day of baseball in my life.

On the first day of soccer practice my dad came home from work and gave me a brand-new pair of white pleather soccer cleats and yellow tube socks that stretched well onto my mid-thigh. Pleather is underrated. I'm pretty sure my first car was made entirely of pleather. So was the family room couch and the jacket I wore to my eighth-grade school dance.

17

I had never played an organized sport, so things like uniforms, referees, and even the coach seemed like nonessentials at the time. Actually, I think all the dads got together five minutes before the first practice to play paper-rock-scissors to see who should coach the team—and apparently my dad lost, because he was my first soccer coach.

I remember the moment I hopped out of my dad's VW Bus, proudly wearing my white pleather cleats, and saw soccer for the first time. I watched the game as if it was the Apollo 11 launch and a new world was just being discovered. I saw other kids dressed in pleather; they were running, screaming, and kicking each other for fun. It seemed like a no-brainer—I decided in that moment that I would be a soccer player. At age five I didn't know what it meant to be a soccer player, but it looked like fun so I committed. I've noticed that often you don't need a plan or strategic goals to pursue something; you just need to decide—*I'm in.*

I attended college but it wasn't based on academic merit, it was to play soccer. When I arrived on campus for preseason, three weeks before classes began, I hadn't given much thought to what else might be involved.

Our first game that season was against one of our school's big rivals. I thought it was a big deal, not because of the opponent but because the coach told me I was going to play. My entire family drove to campus to watch the game. I could tell you that after all these years I can't remember the score, or that it didn't matter anyway, but I would be lying. We won. Good guys 3, bad guys 0.

After that first game I rode my newly purchased yellow 1956 collegiate edition Schwinn bicycle directly from the soccer stadium back to my dorm room. My parents followed me in their car. I figured they would stop their car in front of my dorm just long enough to say "good game" and "good-bye." But apparently they wanted to come in.

My dad decided to wait in the car, but my mom seemed enthusiastic about a guided dorm tour, so in we went. I think most students were off campus, or busy doing whatever it is that college kids do on the weekend. I was relieved. In fact, everything was going according to plan until Mom decided to take my dirty laundry home to be washed. The conversation went something like this:

Mom: "So how's college so far?"

Me: "Fine."

Mom: "Just fine?"

Me: "Yeah . . . fine."

Mom: "Anything exciting happen yet?"

Me: "Not that I can think of."

Then, just as Mom said, "Ok, well, I guess I'll get your laundry and head home," my dorm room door thrust open, inadvertently concealing my mother who was now standing in the closet collecting my laundry. Like a perfectly scripted scene from *Baywatch*, a beautiful but skimpily dressed coed, who happened to be my next-door neighbor, bounded into my room in her bikini with the unbridled enthusiasm of all nineteen-year-old sorority girls. It happened fast. Like a tornado. She was screaming something about happiness and winning soccer games. There was a lot of squealing, bouncing, and hugging involved. Apparently it's also standard practice for sorority gals to kiss one's face repeatedly when offering any form of congratulations. When "bikini girl," as my mom called her for several months following, finally left the room, my hair looked like it had just been through a NASA wind tunnel and red lipstick marks covered my face. The only sound was a soft chuckle coming from behind the door, where Mom still stood. I suppose there wasn't much more to say. As she walked out of my dorm room, holding a basket full of laundry, she turned and said, "So, college is just . . . *fine?*" I smiled and said, "Yeah . . . fine."

At the conclusion of that first college season I won an award for soccer. The award was important to me. I felt it validated my hard work, effort, and sacrifice—even more, I felt it validated *me*, because my dream from that first day of soccer was to earn a scholarship and win *that* specific award. As I stood on the stage to receive the award, I was as proud as I had ever been. For several days following I walked around my college campus with my chest inflated, head up and hands out, as everyone who passed by me offered exuberant congratulations and a swift high five. I felt an overwhelming sense of fulfillment; I was happy.

Winning that award was everything I imagined it might be— for three days. On day four I woke up and the feeling was gone. The trophy was still there but the feeling was not. I had accomplished one of my biggest life goals, but the payoff didn't seem equal to the effort it took to achieve it. After a few days people stopped congratulating me. The excitement diminished. It was as if everyone but me had forgotten the magnitude of my accomplishment. And now, instead of walking around campus with my chest out and head up, I felt empty inside. That experience made me think, *There must be something more.*

I decided to begin a search for something more than soccer. Up until that moment soccer was everything to me. Soccer was my vision. Soccer was my purpose. Soccer was my identity. I had given my life to soccer and I couldn't imagine that there was anything more meaningful or fulfilling, but since soccer didn't ultimately provide everything I had always believed it would, I decided a search was necessary.

I started my search by looking in some books. That might seem like a logical starting point, but I am embarrassed to admit that I had never willingly read a book prior to that time. So I chose a few at random. My only criteria was that the books have the word *Christian* in the title. Since I didn't know anything about most religions and I had grown up going to a Christian church, I figured I should start by investigating the claims of Jesus. I had always thought of myself as a Christian, but it didn't take long to realize that I had absolutely no idea what Jesus was about, who he was, or what he actually stood for.

Sitting in my dorm room one evening in January, I officially launched my search. I felt like a loser sitting alone in my dorm room about to read a book while all of my friends were out having fun, but I needed to know if there was something more meaningful than soccer. I had never heard of the book I chose to read, but it seemed thin enough. I had never heard of the author, C. S. Lewis, either. At the time, my only concern was that it met my criteria—the title was *Mere Christianity*.

I began reading about six o'clock. To my surprise, I didn't stop. I couldn't stop. I didn't eat, drink, or even break for the bathroom—I just read, like a machine. It was probably five or six o'clock the next morning when I finished. I can't say that I comprehended most of what the author wrote about, but one thing seemed clear—Jesus was inviting me to awake to a relationship with him, to experience a life of meaning, purpose, and fulfillment that soccer and every other pursuit to that point had failed to provide.

As the sun rose that morning, I prayed one of the first prayers I can remember. I wasn't sure how I should pray or what I should pray for, so I just talked to Jesus like we were friends. I was on my dorm room floor in what I thought to be a prayer posture—on my knees, forehead on the floor, hands out, and palms up.

"Hey, Jesus, this is Aaron Tredway." I figured a formal introduction might be necessary after years of minimal contact, and I prayed out loud, trying my best not to wake up my roommate, who had stumbled his way into the room sometime around three in the morning. I continued, "Jesus, I've decided . . . I will follow you." I should have stopped there, but I continued. "I only have three conditions and I'm in: one, I don't want to be a pastor, two, I don't want to be a missionary, and three, I don't want to speak in public." I closed with a hearty "Amen," and that was it. No fireworks. No angels. No trumpet sound or heavenly songs—just a simple prayer accepting an outrageous invitation that opened the door to meaning, fulfillment, purpose, and an outrageous life I had never considered possible.

It turns out that college was more than just *fine*, and it had nothing (ok, very little) to do with bikini girl. I started college with a subconscious belief that soccer was the only thing I needed to provide meaning, identity, and purpose in my life. I realize soccer might not be your thing. Perhaps your thing is singing, dancing, academics, or film. Your thing could be any number of things; you might not even know *your thing*, but regardless, I believe Jesus offers you the same invitation he offered me in my college dorm room—it's an invitation to connect your life to his and experience an outrageous life impossible to comprehend without him.

I always thought soccer was my thing, but now I know it was God's thing all along. God has used soccer in my life to open countless doors, create opportunities, and provide some adventures I can only call outrageous. Many of the experiences I have had, and speak about in this book, are connected in some way to my continued involvement in soccer. Soccer certainly isn't my message, but it's definitely the vehicle God has used to shape me, refine me, and move me to the most remarkable places, even to Timbuktu.

My soccer career began when I was five years old with a decision involving two simple words—*I'm in*. Roughly sixteen years, four months, twenty-seven days, eight hours, and several minutes after I wore my first pair of pleather cleats and knee-high yellow tube socks (not that I was counting), soccer was no longer just a passion; it became my profession. It seems that God loves to use our greatest passions, talents, abilities, and interests to accomplish his outrageous purposes in our life—and also in the world. Apparently you don't need an elaborate plan or strategic goals to accept God's invitation to access the outrageous life he desires for you. You just need to decide. God does the rest.

I don't know about you, but I want to awake to God's invitation to an outrageous life, and that's why I've decided—*I'm in*.

2

SON OF THE KING

"JESUS, *HELP ME*." I didn't have time for any formalities. That was the best I could do as the anxious crowd scurried along the tarmac, pushing their way toward the customs entrance.

As I approached, aggressively being pushed from behind, I noticed a woman standing off to the side. She was a calm within the storm as she stood peacefully holding a single white piece of paper in front of her chest. I couldn't help but be curious. She was exquisite. I make no excuses.

I didn't want to stare, but I shot another quick glance her way. I was sure she didn't notice.

Now, as I prepared to enter the customs building, something clicked in my brain. That single white piece of paper the woman was holding said: "Señor Aaron." It seems ridiculous but I thought to myself, *Hey, wait, my name is Aaron!*

I attempted to suppress the immediate and overwhelming urge to sprint toward the woman to acknowledge myself as *an* "Aaron," thinking of course, I was definitely not *the* Aaron this fine-looking woman was searching for. After all, this was my first visit to Mozambique and I only knew one person. It wasn't her.

———

That was the scene the day I arrived in Mozambique without my passport.

I know what you are thinking. *How is that possible? How was he permitted to check his baggage, collect his boarding pass, exit a country, and board a flight to a different country . . . with NO PASSPORT?*

I can only say it happened.

And by the time I realized the oversight, I couldn't turn back. That's when I prayed, "Jesus, *help me.*" It wasn't a profound prayer. It probably wouldn't have impressed my New Testament seminary professor, or my third-grade Awana leader for that matter, but I had no plan B.

I intended to walk into the customs building, approach the inevitably grumpy customs agent, and promptly be shipped back to where I came from.

I knew the drill. You simply do not enter a foreign country without the proper identification.

———

Sometimes I wonder what might have happened if I had made a different choice. What if I had patiently waited my turn with everyone else? What if I had controlled my curiosity and parked my intrigue on the side of the tarmac?

But I had to know.

I had to say something.

So, as the masses streamed past the exquisite woman holding the single white piece of paper, I fought my way toward her and extracted myself from the surging convoy. Standing just three feet from her, I rallied all my courage and attempted an introduction.

"Hello." Long, awkward pause. "I am." Even longer, more awkward pause. "Um. I'm *Aaron*."

I'm not sure if she had spent the morning rehearsing her response in the mirror, but she immediately dropped her designer handbag onto the tarmac, raised both hands above her head, and exclaimed, "Señor Aaron, Velcom to Mozambique!"

I was confident that I could not be the "Señor Aaron" this woman hoped to find, but somewhere between my curiosity and her enthusiastically kissing me multiple times on each cheek, I decided I would just go with it.

From that moment things shifted into hyper speed.

Somehow we managed to bypass all the customs formalities, and the woman quickly ushered me through a side door that I deduced was labeled "private" through my limited Portuguese language skills.

Now I was standing inside a room that I can only equate to a setting from the 1972 cult classic *The Godfather*, yet this scene was not being directed by Francis Ford Coppola and Al Pacino was nowhere in sight. The room was dimly lit and the air was damp, filled with a lingering mix of musty cigar ash and whiskey. Fat, bearded men sat on small chairs grumbling about their cheating friends and the validity of the last throw of the dice.

We walked through the room and then entered the main airport terminal, where a slightly thinner bearded man appeared with my suitcase.

How did we bypass customs?

How did the man get my suitcase?

How did he know that suitcase was mine?

Walking through the airport terminal, I began to notice people. Normal people. Janitors. Businesspeople. Airline employees. There was nothing exceptional about these people, except their behavior.

As I passed a janitor he bowed facedown to the floor.

As I passed a businessman he bowed facedown to the floor.

All the airline employees bowed facedown to the floor.

I thought to myself, *Who is this Señor Aaron? Why are these people prostrating themselves on the floor?* I wanted to scream, "Get up! Stop that! I'm not who you think I am!"

But just as quickly as we had entered the terminal, we departed. Outside the airport another bearded man sat waiting in a car. Apparently he was our driver.

The bearded man started the car, shifted into gear, and accelerated toward us as if his life depended on it. I'm sure this guy was moonlighting, taking time off from the Formula One circuit. He spoke no English but his expressive gesticulation suggested that I should get into the backseat.

So there we were. The woman who had been holding the piece of paper, the thinner bearded bag man, the bearded driver . . . and *me*.

If there was ever a time for one's imagination to take over, this was it. Driving through the streets of the capital of Mozambique, a town called Maputo, I kept thinking that I no longer wanted to be Señor Aaron. I've noticed this happens sometimes: the person we hope to be is not the person we are supposed to be.

I decided that Señor Aaron must be a very bad man. I could only conclude that he must be a mafia boss or a drug lord, and whatever business he was there to conduct, it wasn't going to be good.

The phone rang.

"Ah-lo?" said the exquisite woman in the front seat.

Turning toward me, she extended the phone and said, "Eet's for jew!"

I slowly pulled the phone to my ear and heard a monotone voice ask, "Is everything all right?" I didn't recognize the voice, but the question was delivered in perfect English.

"Who is this?" I yelled.

The voice was unfazed. "I asked if everything is all right?"

"Um. Well. Maybe. I guess. Yes. I think everything is all right," I said.

The voice seemed pleased. "Good. I will see you soon."

Moments later we whipped into the parking lot of what appeared to be a bathroom tile store. I thought to myself, *I knew it! Bad stuff always happens in parking lots. This is where it all goes down.*

To my surprise, the only person I knew in Mozambique walked out of the tile store, greeted the woman in the front seat with multiple cheek kisses, and then walked around the car to greet me.

He didn't have time to say a word, because I began spewing the events of the preceding hour—the woman with the sign, the gambling, bearded men from *The Godfather*, the people bowing down, and my underlying fear of impending doom.

My friend laughed more than necessary.

He placed his hand on my shoulder and said, "I thought you might need some help entering Mozambique, so I called someone."

Motioning toward the woman in the front seat, he said, "She works as the personal attaché to the president of Mozambique. This morning, during her routine meeting with the president, she told him that the son of a king would arrive in Mozambique today."

It was so ridiculous I don't think I could process it.

"She said what?" I asked.

My friend said again, "She said *you* are the *son of a king*."

Immediate thoughts of extradition, public humiliation, and imprisonment for international fraud, among other related criminal acts, filled my head.

Perhaps she didn't realize that I lived in Ohio. I had a mortgage. I took my wife to McDonald's for her last birthday (a shameful but true reality).

After collecting my thoughts for a moment, all I could muster is, "Why would she lie? I'm obviously not the son of a king!"

My friend laughed to himself some more. Then he said, "She didn't lie—she just didn't mention which King you are the son of."

I learned an important lesson that day in Mozambique about who I am and who I am supposed to be. Most days I feel more *ordinary* than anything. I don't sail on yachts or collect rare vintage cars or fly in private jets. I own a few suits, but I don't usually wear them. I'm not exactly sure how you become a king if you aren't born into it, or whom I would call to find out, but that day in Mozambique my friend told me that's exactly what I am—the son of a king.

Any day prior to that one, if you had asked me about who I am, I'm sure I would have responded, "I'm just a normal guy from a normal town who leads a fairly normal life." But I realized that day—God has invited me to something more.

In the book of Ephesians, the apostle Paul says that *God chose us to be adopted as his sons and daughters through Jesus.*[1] So even though we might not look like, talk like, act like, or even feel like royalty, Jesus has invited us to become children of God—who is *the King.*

1. See Ephesians 1:5.

I've realized that although it doesn't seem natural for me to think of myself as a son of a king, that's the invitation God has to offer. We get to choose how we respond to the invitation and also what we do with this outrageous position we receive. The opportunities, possibilities, and even adventures that arise as a result of our identity in Jesus might extend beyond the ordinary. But it makes sense. We aren't just children of *a* king—our Father is *the* King!

It might seem outrageous, but I want to awake to the identity that God has offered me so that I can leverage my position as a son of the king for all that God has created me to do.

3

LETTERS HOME

"Do you know al-Bashir?" That was the first thing my friend said when I answered the phone a few years ago.

"Al-who?" I responded.

"Omar Hassan Ahmad al-Bashir, the president of Sudan."

I had never heard of President al-Bashir before that phone call, but apparently he had heard of me. My friend, who will remain nameless for safety purposes, said, "The president wants you to come to Sudan!"

I couldn't imagine why the president of Sudan, or any country for that matter, would want *me* to visit their country. I'm not a political figure. I have no government involvement, either foreign or domestic. I barely know the names of the current US presidential candidates. I'm no one that any world leader should be concerned about meeting, but al-Bashir loves soccer and he was looking for a team from the West to play a match in Khartoum, the capital of Sudan, as a gesture of peace and goodwill between the nations. And my friend had told the president I could help.

"So, what do you think about the president's invitation?" my friend asked as our conversation was concluding.

In hindsight, I probably should have considered the fact that Sudan had been involved in a civil war for over twenty years, the country was on the United Nations blacklist, and al-Bashir was well known for his indignation toward the West, especially toward those who claim to follow Jesus. But for whatever reason, I didn't. With almost no hesitation, I responded, "I'll go." And that was it. The deal was done. The question was, who would go with me?

The first person I called was Shak. Growing up, Shak dreamed of playing soccer at UCLA, so when he graduated from high school and didn't receive a scholarship offer, he decided to "walk on" to the UCLA team anyway. Shak never played a game his freshman year, but he was always the first one at practice and the last one to leave. And when the season ended, Shak decided to practice even harder.

During the first game of Shak's sophomore year, UCLA was playing their rival, Santa Clara University. Shak wasn't on the field, but he was happy just to have a spot on the team. About ten minutes into the game, the senior, All-American captain of UCLA got injured. Shak always sat at the very end of the bench, and that's exactly where he was when the coach of UCLA looked past every other player that day and yelled, "Shak . . . *you're in!*" UCLA won the college national championship that year. Shak never sat on the bench again.

I asked Shak to come to the Sudan because somewhere sandwiched between his college national championship trophy, his bronze medal in the Pan-American Games, and his opportunity to play in the Olympics, Shak encountered Jesus and began to awaken to a completely new paradigm and focus for his life. Up until he connected his life to Jesus, Shak was all about himself. He believed his purpose was to make his own name famous. He lived for his own glory.

Despite his college success, Shak didn't expect to become a professional player. In fact, the day before the college draft in Fort Lauderdale, Florida, Shak was hanging out with some friends when a sports agent called him and told him he'd better be in Fort Lauderdale by morning. The next day Shak got dressed in the only suit he owned and a pair of dress shoes he borrowed from his brother. He sat unassumingly somewhere in the middle of the large crowd gathered to witness the Major League Soccer draft. Shak didn't expect to be selected by a team; he was just happy to have been invited.

New York had the first selection in the draft that year. It was also the first year that ESPN produced a live broadcast of the event. As the broadcast started and the draft began, the league commissioner promptly stepped up to the podium, welcomed the viewing audience, and said, "I will now announce the first pick in the 2000 MLS draft." There were a lot of highly regarded players in the draft that year, so there had been a lot of speculation about who would become the number-one pick.

That day, in that room, televised for the entire world to see, the MLS league commissioner stood at the podium and said, "With the first pick of the draft New York chooses . . . Shak." The crowd applauded. The media waited. Shak didn't move. The commissioner said again, "With the first pick of the draft New

York chooses . . . Shak!" And then he added, "Shak, please come to the podium." Shak still didn't move. Apparently Shak was so surprised to hear his name called first, let alone called at all, that he didn't believe it could be true.

When Shak finally got to the podium, he was completely unprepared. The commissioner held up a black-and-red striped jersey with his name on the back, put a team scarf around his neck (it's a soccer thing), and said, "Shak, congratulations, *you* are the number-one MLS draft pick. Do you have anything you want to say?" Shak stood motionless, staring out across the crowd of his peers, live on ESPN, and after a long period of silence, he said, without any reluctance, apprehension, or hesitation, "As I stand here today I realize everything I have ever had, everything I have now, and everything I hope to have in the future comes from Jesus alone. Thank you." And in that moment Shak decided the pursuit of his own glory was far less significant than the pursuit of the glory of God.

Shak, I, and fifteen other professional soccer players from different teams flew to Johannesburg, South Africa, en route to Khartoum, Sudan, two months after we received the invitation from President al-Bashir. I don't think any of us had any idea what we were in for.

In order to prepare, we spent a week in South Africa and Mozambique visiting orphanages and schools and playing practice matches against local teams. Everyone knew that Sudan was our ultimate goal, but we were caught up in the activities of the moment.

The day before our scheduled flight from Johannesburg to Khartoum, the team gathered at a small guest lodge for a final meeting. We sat on the green grass in the guest lodge courtyard, bathed by the warm South African sun. The air was crisp and the sky was clear. The mood was jovial. But that would quickly change.

That afternoon the friend who had originally called me to share al-Bashir's invitation requested a meeting with the team to set expectations and discuss some of the scenarios we might encounter in Sudan. He was initially enthusiastic, appreciative, and complimentary of our willingness to visit Sudan, but he wanted to make sure we understood the reality of the situation. He spoke for over one hour straight. No one moved. No one else spoke. I don't know if guys were even breathing after my friend began the discussion by saying, "Tomorrow, when you land in Khartoum, you could die."

He spoke about the ongoing civil war and the commonality of seeing people with missing fingers, toes, or entire limbs because of wartime tactics and the immediacy of the fighting. He also spoke about different terrorist groups. At that time, eight of the top ten largest terrorist organizations were possibly headquartered in Khartoum. And if that wasn't enough, he suggested the general public disposition toward the West, especially toward followers of Jesus, was one of animosity and aggressive hostility.

After about an hour a member of the team reluctantly raised his hand and sheepishly asked, "So, are you saying we shouldn't go?"

I know I was the catalyst for most of the guys who had volunteered to participate in this outrageous adventure to Sudan, but as I was sitting there hearing my friend talk candidly about the risk we were taking and the hostility we would likely encounter, I secretly hoped he would tell us, "Don't go!" or "Don't be crazy!" or "You have too much to lose!" But he didn't.

He just sat there. He didn't respond. He didn't say anything for what seemed like an eternity. And then, with tears in his eyes, he finally said, "Is Jesus worthy?"

Worthy of what? I immediately thought to myself.

All the guys sitting on the grass under the South African sun that day had left the comforts of home, family, friends, children—we had sacrificed to go to Sudan. But the question wasn't about what we had or had not sacrificed—the question was: Is Jesus worthy of our sacrifice?

As we all sat there silently contemplating his question, my friend dropped a final bomb on the team. He said, "If you are committed to going to Khartoum tomorrow, I am going to require that you write a letter to your friends and family explaining why you decided to sacrifice your life for Jesus." Have you ever seen fifteen manly men weep and wail like babies? That was the scene immediately following that request.

Amid the emotion of the moment, my friend repeatedly said, "There will be no shame or judgment if you decide not to go to Sudan, but if you decide to go I want your letter as a testimony of your decision." Several more guys started crying when he said, "Tomorrow I will collect the letters and store them together in a lockbox in the Johannesburg airport. Should anything happen, and if for whatever reason you do not return from Sudan, your letter will be personally delivered to whomever you request."

As the guys began to disperse to make their final decisions and write their letters I noticed Shak sitting with his head in his hands. He would later tell me that he had decided that same day to ask his girlfriend to marry him. What if something happened to him in Sudan? Was he to sacrifice his future with her and go to Khartoum?

I didn't go back to my room. Actually, I didn't move from where I was sitting. I just closed my eyes, lay down on the grass, and thought about my life; I thought about everything I had, my hopes and dreams for the future, my family, and the enormous sacrifice it would be if I went to Sudan and didn't return.

———

The thing about writing a letter like that is it's precautionary; it will likely never be read. But that doesn't make it any less real. What everyone realized that afternoon while sitting on the grass in the cool breeze under the warm South African sun is that the only way to write the letter was to first answer the question *Is Jesus worthy of my life?*

As I lay on the grass with my eyes closed, I made a decision. *I can't go. I won't go. It's too risky.* But just as I was about to open my eyes and share my decision, I remembered something Jesus said: "Whoever wants to save their life will lose it, but whoever loses their life for me will find it."[2] All of a sudden I thought to myself, *Wait, maybe it's actually more risky if I don't go.* Jesus was clear—if we really want to find our life we must be prepared to lose it.

———

That afternoon every person on the team wrote a letter. I'm sure every letter contained different sentiments, thoughts, and words, but ultimately each letter decisively proclaimed the same thing—*Jesus is worthy of my life!*

The next morning everyone got on the plane to Sudan. When we arrived in Khartoum, we were welcomed on the runway by several members of parliament, national media, and a full brass band. Everywhere the team traveled, four hundred armed guards and a ten-car motorcade escorted us. Dignitaries, politicians, and even President al-Bashir spent time with us.

2. See Matthew 16:25; Mark 8:35; and Luke 9:24.

On the final day we played the Sudan national soccer team in the national stadium in front of thousands of people. As we drove into the stadium, I knew that if something were going to happen, it would likely be there. Walking onto the field, Shak said, "You know it would only take one crazy person with a pipe bomb who wanted to send a message today." I couldn't disagree. Though the game was called a friendly match, the environment in the stadium was tense. People were waving their arms and yelling aggressively in Arabic. And then, just before halftime, the game was officially stopped as the entire stadium responded to a call to prayer over the loudspeaker. Every person left their seat, walked onto the field, got on their hands and knees, and worshiped their god together for five minutes.

At halftime I was approached by Al Jazeera, the largest Islamic news organization, which broadcasts in over eighty countries around the world. A reporter asked if I would do a live interview. Given the setting, it didn't seem like a good idea to me. I was petrified of the potential outcome, but I had a choice to make—was I willing to awake to the outrageous opportunity before me or not? So, standing there on the sideline of the field with the reporter and an underground pastor who quickly volunteered to be my translator, the reporter said, "I have just one question. Why have you come to Sudan?"

It was a live interview, so I didn't have much time to think. I immediately looked at the underground pastor, who looked back at me, nodded, and then subtly pumped his fist, as if to say—*tell them!*

Why did we leave our children? Why did we leave our wives? Why did we leave our houses, cars, and the comforts of home? Why did we write those letters and get on that plane? *Why did we go to Sudan?* Then, on live television, while millions of Muslims around the world were watching, these words came out of my mouth: "His name is *Jesus*. He's the reason we came. He's the only one who has sacrificed more than we could ever give."

For months following the trip, we received letters, emails, and text messages from people around the world who had watched the game on Al Jazeera, heard our testimony about Jesus's outrageous love, and wrote to say, "Now I know. God has not forgotten me!"

Now I don't know about you, but I want to awake to Jesus, who is worthy of my life. After all, you never know what invitations you might receive.

4

STOLEN

MY FRIEND KENT used to love moccasin shoes. For at least ten years he refused to wear any footwear aside from his one pair of prized brown moccasins. For some reason those moccasins always irritated me. The more Kent wore them, the more I believed they had to go.

One day I plotted the moccasins' demise. At first I tried backing over them with my car, but they survived. Next I dug a hole and hid them in my backyard, but the dog found them. Then I asked a pair of Mormon missionaries who came to my door if they would take them, but they couldn't carry them on their bikes. No matter what I tried, I couldn't get rid of those moccasins! I even put them in the Salvation Army Christmas gift bag at the mall—somehow those shoes always returned.

A few years ago Kent, his moccasins, and I decided to go on vacation. We thought of the idea on a Tuesday and by Friday we were in Milan, Italy. At the time, Kent and I were both single and working for a nonprofit organization, earning much less than a livable wage. We didn't have much discretionary income but we had some airline miles, free time, and a bag of beef jerky, so we figured we might as well go.

I am normally the type of person who likes to plan for spontaneity, but over the years I've noticed that life often serves up some of the most outrageous opportunities, events, and adventures when you leave the script behind.

Kent and I chose to go to Italy for one reason: *coffee*. Sure, there's great food, wine, history, culture, architecture, and a host of other compelling reasons to visit Italy, but no one does coffee like the Italians. Coffee is not a morning beverage or an afternoon pick-me-up to an Italian; it's an art form. Coffee is tradition, friendship, community, and a daily event. Italians don't wake up and fill their twelve-ounce to-go mugs with home-brewed Folger's crystals before rushing out the front door to tackle the day—they meet, talk, debate, and celebrate life in the form of perfectly crafted espresso shots each morning in their local coffee bar. That's what Kent and I were seeking—culture, with a little crème on top.

We arrived in Milan just as the sun was rising. There was no time to waste—the coffee was calling us. After finding our luggage, we thought about taking the train into the city, but as we were walking through the airport we noticed a sign for "Rent-a-Cheapie." I liked the company's name. I liked their slogan even better: "Cars for any budget." Within thirty minutes, we had rented a car slightly larger than my briefcase and were off on our great Italian adventure.

Driving down the A8 toward the center of Milan, Kent and I were like two gorillas stuffed into a circus sidecar, but it didn't matter—we were in Italy! We were young, single, and full of life—and full of ourselves.

Although we were sitting three inches from each other in our briefcase-sized car, we kept looking at each other and yelling everything we said.

Me: "Kent . . . We. Are. In. *Italy!*"

Kent: "Dude, this is awesome!"

Me: "We must be two of the most spontaneous people on earth!"

Kent: "We totally are! We're like extreme explorers in search of hidden coffee treasure!"

There were also several animated high fives and fist bumps being thrown around. In our excitement we even used the old-fashioned hand cranks to roll down the windows of our Rent-a-Cheapie. Kent stuck his head out the window and began yelling things like, "Carpe diem!" "Veni, vidi, vici!" and other things that most Europeans would imagine only obnoxious American tourists might say, including, "Vive la Italy!" I didn't have the heart to tell him that's a *French* expression.

It took about one hour to drive into central Milan; our first stop was a no-brainer—Café Milano. We had heard the most famous street in Milan was Corso Buenos Aires, so that's where we went. We arrived at about eight in the morning. To our surprise, there was almost no one around. We learned later that it was the first day of the Catholic holiday the Feast of the Assumption—a big deal in the country that is home to the Vatican.

Since there was almost no one on the Corso Buenos Aires that morning, we easily found parking. The stars had aligned and we were being rewarded for our spontaneity. At least that was how we felt as we jumped out of the car, locked its doors, and began sprinting toward our first Italian coffee like schoolkids at the sound of the classroom bell.

The next fifteen minutes were exactly as we had envisioned. The café was filled with chic Milanese men wearing skinny jeans and slim-fit button-down shirts, long before skinny jeans and slim-fit button-down shirts had been conceived, or even remotely considered to be cool, anywhere outside of Europe. Most were smoking thin cigarettes and speaking as if they were acting out an intense scene from *Phantom of the Opera* on Broadway. No one sat down. Everyone was leaning on a waist-high bar in front of two beautiful bronze espresso machines. The bar was full of cigarette ash and miniature white porcelain coffee cups that held a maximum of a double espresso shot. Kent and I laughed as we stood at the bar, drinking in our surroundings and several shots of espresso.

Most of the shops and cafés were closed for the Feast of the Assumption, so after we had finished our espresso we decided we were also finished with Milan. Unfortunately, we didn't realize that Milan was not finished with us.

Monaco is only a three-hour drive from Milan, so we figured we could be there by lunchtime—or at least by dinner, as the toaster posing as our car topped out at about forty-eight miles per hour.

Everything seemed to be going according to plan. About ninety minutes into our drive, Kent and I were cruising along the freeway, energized by the residual caffeine buzz and some pulsating Italian rave music on the radio. That's when I asked him to grab my sunglasses from the trunk. I should have known something wasn't right when he crawled into the backseat and didn't return.

After some time, I noticed Kent was still fumbling around in the backseat, so I turned down the music and yelled, "Hey, man, what's happening with those sunglasses?" Kent didn't say anything. I yelled again, "Hey, it's pretty bright out here; a pair of sunglasses would definitely help!" Kent still didn't respond. I decided to pull over.

Kent didn't seem to be incapacitated or physically debilitated in any way, but when I got out of the car and opened the back door, he was peering under the removable, felt-coated hatchback cover into the trunk. I said, "Hey, man, you ok?"

"Yeah, but I think we have a problem."

"What's the problem?"

"I can't see our bags?"

I wasn't sure if that was a question, a statement, or a metaphor. So I said, "Where do you think our bags are?"

"I don't know, but they aren't here!"

We searched that shoebox-sized trunk for at least fifteen minutes, hoping our bags would miraculously appear. Oddly, they did not. We retraced our every step, from the airport, to the rental car desk, to the car, to Corso Buenos Aires—we definitely *had* our bags, but we didn't have them now. The only logical scenario was that someone must have broken into our car during the twenty minutes we were sipping our espresso, but then also considerately locked the car doors when they left.

We decided our only option was to return to the scene of the crime. We had been gone for over three hours when we arrived back at the café, and despite our best effort, our bags were nowhere to be found. We filed a police report. We went back to the airport. We even drove around the city, thinking we might see a thief pulling our suitcases down the street. Unfortunately, our bags were gone.

I think there are several benefits to being young, single, and full of life, but that afternoon we realized there is also a potential problem. When everything you own can fit into a carry-on bag, what happens if someone steals that bag?

The remaining details of our spontaneous Italian adventure are fairly uninspiring. We spent almost a week in Milan waiting for the Feast of the Assumption to end so we could get new passports. In the meantime we made a collect call to our families in the United States and had just enough money wired to us to buy a few pairs of underwear and some toothpaste, and to cover our hotel until we could go home.

Italy wasn't the experience I had anticipated or hoped for, but I did learn a valuable lesson in the process. When I returned home and began replacing everything I had previously owned— wallet, driver's license, laptop, cell phone, clothes, shoes, even my Bible—I realized that all the *stuff* I have can be stolen, but it's impossible to steal my joy, zeal, or passion for life because they are rooted in my faith in Jesus. Yes, it was extremely disappointing and aggravating to lose most of my worldly possessions, but Italy helped me realize my possessions don't enable or provide access to the outrageous life God wants for me—only Jesus provides that.

I've realized my faith in Jesus provides a secure foundation for my life that releases me to be more spontaneous, adventurous, and willing to move toward potentially outrageous circumstances, because no matter what happens, no matter where I go, no matter who I meet, no matter what I experience, and even no matter what gets stolen from me along the way—my faith in Jesus remains the same.

You can steal my Bible but you can't steal my faith. And apparently you can't steal Kent's moccasins either—aside from the clothes on our backs, those shoes were the only thing we retained.

5

STOVI STARS

I USED TO DIRECT a professional soccer team. Two friends and I founded the Cleveland City Stars because we wanted to create a platform to *be* the church in our city. For a long time I thought the church was a place of gathering, or a building, but the church is more about people than it is about a structure. People gather. People worship. People fellowship. Buildings do not. The church is a group of people who rally around the death, burial, and resurrection of Jesus, and seek to connect with other people in tangible ways with the hope of Jesus practically demonstrated. My two friends and I founded the Cleveland City Stars because we believed we could be the church through soccer.

When we founded the Cleveland City Stars we didn't have a clue what we were doing. Our pooled resources included some soccer experience and two life-sized sumo-wrestling suits we had bought in an online auction.

At the time Cleveland was classified as the poorest city in America. The urban area was rough, and it didn't appear to be getting any better. Our vision had started one day when my friend said, "What if we had a soccer team that sought to win games on the field and serve people off the field?" I liked that idea. I started to dream about what it would be like to gather a group of like-minded people who wanted to make a difference in our city by serving as role models to urban youth by connecting with kids each week through different after-school programs. It wasn't the standard vision for a professional sports team, but it was our goal. We wanted to serve our city through soccer.

The Cleveland City Stars were like any start-up company; we had to create *everything* . . . now! At first it seemed fun. It energized us to choose colors, logos, business cards, and letterhead, but that thrill didn't last long. After a few weeks, our decision making began to look something like this: as we were sitting around a small table in Starbucks, someone said, "Ok, next agenda item: team mascot."

"What are the options?"

Silence.

"What about a crocodile?"

Everyone around the table laughed out loud.

"A crocodile? Why would Cleveland have a crocodile mascot?!"

Silence.

Blank stares.

More silence.

"Ok, so everyone agrees on the crocodile as the mascot?"

Everyone nodded. *Yes*.

With only three weeks until the start of the inaugural Cleveland City Stars season, things weren't going as we had envisioned. We were headquartered in a barn and had only six of the needed twenty-six players, some letterhead, and a gigantic crocodile suit. I wish I was making this up, but the best player we were scouting was a guy from Nigeria named Harry Toe. Oddly, Harry didn't seem to understand why we laughed every time he called the office and said, "Hello, this is Harry Toe!"

With each passing day our small leadership team became more nervous about our impending catastrophic failure. I kept thinking, *What made us think we could start a professional soccer team? We clearly don't know what we are doing!* We didn't have nearly enough financial backing, we had no uniforms, we had only limited sponsorship, and almost every player we contacted about joining our team said, "*Cleveland . . . not interested.*"

One afternoon my two friends and I were meeting at an indoor training facility called The Edge. We were feeling desperate and overwhelmed by our ludicrous decision to operate a professional soccer team. We were destined to fail. I suggested, "We could call the league and tell them we made a mistake." No one thought that would work. In fact, we couldn't collectively think of one idea that would assist our cause. That is, until someone suggested, "Maybe we should pray?" I've noticed, in moments like that, when we feel inadequate and unable, we can choose to throw in the towel or awaken to God's power and authority, which is always much greater than our own.

It's funny; our vision for the team was to create a platform to be the church in our city, but until that moment it seemed we had left God out of the equation. We got on our hands and knees and prayed. *God, you have brought us to The Edge. We acknowledge today we can't do this alone; only you are able!* It would have been miraculous, but as we prayed the heavens didn't part. No doves descended from on high. No one received any grand revelation. But we did experience a new sense of peace that God was in control.

The next day was the start of a two-week tryout. Several hundred hopeful players came to Cleveland to participate. Week one was open to any player who registered. Week two was by invitation only. While the players all flew in, I flew out. I returned home one week later, the day before the invitational tryout began.

I arrived in Cleveland about five in the afternoon, collected my luggage, found my car in the airport parking garage, and drove home. I knew the following day would be full of activity, so I was looking forward to a shower, some food, and an early night. That's not what happened.

At the time, I was single and living alone, so it was quite a shock when I drove onto my street and noticed six cars parked in my driveway. I was new to the neighborhood, but it seemed strange that people would park at my house while I was gone. Regardless, it was late and I was tired, so I decided to park on the street and deal with the issue in the morning. That's when my assistant, Jan, called.

"Welcome home, Aaron!"

"Yes, good, um, Jan . . . quick question—do you know anything about the cars in my driveway?"

"Oh! I forgot to tell you . . ."

"Yes?"

"Don't worry. Those cars belong to some of the players trying out for our team."

"Ok, but why did they park at *my* house?"

"The players are staying at your house."

Apparently Jan thought it would be a good idea to have some of the players stay at my house while I was away, to save money. Have you ever seen National Lampoon's *Animal House*? That was the scene as I walked in my front door. There were empty pizza boxes, music pumping, and guys with their shoes on my furniture, watching my TV, playing my video games, and generally doing whatever they felt like—in *my* house. I stood at the front door in a minor state of shock and awe until one guy yelled from across *my* living room, "Hey man; come on in!" It was a very hospitable gesture.

I didn't have many options so I set my luggage down, walked in, and greeted the half-dressed man who had graciously allowed me to enter *my own house*. He had a huge smile and perfect white teeth. He said, "Hey, are you here for the tryout?" I'm sure I didn't respond, but he said, "Yeah, I'm trying out too!"

This guy was interesting. He was a small but well-built African American with a yellow fauxhawk and a Southern accent. He said his name was Stovi.

For the next two hours Stovi told me pretty much everything about himself, pausing only momentarily to breathe when absolutely necessary. He spoke about his childhood in Atlanta and South Carolina and his love of chicken and waffles, and he kept saying throughout the night, "You know, I'm a *baller!*" I didn't even know what a baller was. I looked it up later online—baller: *someone who's got mad game.*

I must have yawned three hundred times before Stovi got the hint. Long after everyone else had gone to bed, he finally said, "Hey man, big day tomorrow, we'd better get some sleep!" He mentioned a spare bed in *his* room, but I decided to find my own spot.

I woke up early the next morning, partly because of jet lag and partly because I had a meeting. I made some coffee, ate some cereal, put on my best suit, and left the house long before the players woke up.

By the time my meeting finished, the tryout had started. I drove to our borrowed stadium downtown and parked my car. As I entered the building I could feel the nervous energy. The players were running, screaming, and playing as hard as they could to fulfill their dream of becoming professional athletes. I stood in the corner watching for a few minutes, but when the coach noticed me he quickly called me over. He stopped the practice and said, "Guys, we won't stop long, but I want to introduce you to someone very important. This is the executive director and founder of the Cleveland City Stars, Aaron Tredway." You could see the players' eyes widen. They stood tall, wanting to make a good first impression—every player but one, that is.

Stovi was standing in the middle of the group looking directly at the ground, shaking his head, when the coach said, "Aaron, would you like to say anything to the players?"

I said, "Yes, I would!" Now, I must admit, when I was driving to the stadium I thought the coach might introduce me to the players at some point, so I had prepared a little speech. I began, "Guys, welcome to Cleveland! We are thrilled that you want to join us for this inaugural season."

I spoke about our vision to be the church and invest in the lives of urban youth, and how they would become role models to thousands of kids in our city. And then I pointed toward a door and said, "In a few days, some of you will walk through that door into my office and sign a contract to become a professional soccer player for the Cleveland City Stars." As I spoke, I could see the players' eyes widen even more. That was their dream. That was why they were in Cleveland.

But then, surveying the group, I looked directly at Stovi and said, "Unfortunately, not everyone will earn a contract this week." Stovi covered his face with his hands.

That inaugural Cleveland City Stars season wasn't exactly what we had envisioned, but it was exactly what God intended it to be from the beginning. At the end of the tryout week, Stovi walked through my office door and signed a contract. He also became one of the most popular players we had over three seasons. Who knew? I guess he was a *baller* after all.

I saw Stovi a few months ago. He no longer has a yellow faux-hawk, but he still likes to talk. Chatting that night over dinner, he looked at me and said, "Hey, man, do you remember when we met?" I didn't remember, but Stovi did.

He said, "You thought I wasn't going to play for the Cleveland City Stars."

"That's not true. I just wanted you to know that I was going to be the one to make the final decision."

The day I met Stovi, he didn't realize who I was; maybe he didn't fully grasp the authority I had in that particular situation. I've noticed I have a tendency to approach God in the same way that Stovi approached me that day. So often I don't fully realize, recognize, or acknowledge God for who he is.

The Bible describes God as all-powerful and all-knowing, the Creator and sustainer of everything. In the Old Testament there are hundreds of names for God that describe his character; one of my favorite names for God is *El Elyon*—the Most High. I love this name because it identifies God as the One who is in control, the One who presides over all creation. Sometimes I forget that. Sometimes I just don't realize exactly who he is.

My two friends and I would have never anticipated the success of the Cleveland City Stars; we were undefeated our first season and won the national championship our second season. But even more importantly, we were intentional about building friendships, establishing relationships, and being the church among everyone we encountered through soccer.

So I've decided I want to awake to God's authority and ability to accomplish much more than I could hope to accomplish on my own.

6

BEN'S BUNNIES

I OFTEN TELL PEOPLE that I'm an extroverted introvert. I enjoy meeting new people and being part of a group, but I also find it exhausting. My friend Dave feels the same way. Dave spends most of his time in public gatherings, but he likes to say, "I love my own small group. Just me, myself, and I."

A few years ago I moved to Cleveland, Ohio. I think Cleveland gets a bad rap. Sure, it's gray, cold, and covered in snow for more than half the year; most of the sports teams are horrible (Cleveland Cavaliers presently excluded); and someone recently wrote a letter titled, "Open Letter to the City of Cleveland: Stop Sucking," but really, it's not so bad.

One of my favorite ways to spend time is at the gym. No matter where I might be on any given day, I do my best to find some gym time. It's not just good for my body; it's good for my soul—I listen to my favorite music, think about life, and just enjoy some time with *me*. So when I moved to Cleveland, finding a gym was a major priority.

Gyms didn't seem to be as popular as craft beer in Cleveland, but eventually I found one. As gyms go, it was nice. The locker room was clean, the weights were plentiful, and the testosterone was high. I joined immediately.

I must have gone to that gym five or six times every week for over six months. It was my routine. At five o'clock I would depart my office, drive a few miles down the road, and park my car at the gym. I would greet the woman at the front desk, change my clothes in the locker room, and then work out—just me, myself, and I.

One day, in the middle of my workout, I noticed that almost everyone else in the gym had a partner, friend, or someone they spoke with while they were there. I had no one. I wondered, *If Jesus came to the gym, would he keep to himself? Would he have a workout partner? Would he turn up his music and shut out the world?* I assume Jesus would have been fairly social at church, in the office, and perhaps when he walked down the street, but what about a place like the gym?

As I rode the elliptical, it occurred to me that I approached my life in segments and, as a result, I had different expectations depending on the segment. For example, I always viewed the gym as *my time*. But I started to think, *Maybe I'm missing something in the gym—and other places too. Am I missing out on something simply because of the way I approach different scenarios in my life with preconceived expectations?* It wasn't my habit, but I decided to stop, right there in the gym, and pray. *God, do you have something more for me in this gym?*

It turns out he did.

The following day was Easter. I was living with a family in Cleveland at the time. I occupied the downstairs bedroom and everyone else slept upstairs. That was usually a good thing, unless some special event caused the kids to wake up early.

Easter is a special day; particularly when you are two little girls ages eight and eleven and you know you will find large baskets filled with assorted sugary items and magic markers downstairs when you wake up. It was probably five thirty or six in the morning when the girls discovered their Easter treats, conveniently located right outside my bedroom door. I assume the morning began with glee, but by the time I opened my door, that had long since passed. I suppose you can always find something to argue about when you are sisters. Even on Easter morning.

I got out of bed in an attempt to mediate the discussion, largely because I was hoping to go back to sleep should the argument dissipate, but they were committed. Wesley, the younger sister, had received a large pack of temporary Easter tattoos. Apparently she was willing to share with the family dog but not her older sister, Andrea. I walked out of my room into a war zone.

Andrea: "Aaron, Wesley put a tattoo on the dog's tail but she won't give me any!"

Me: blank stare. No response.

Andrea: "Mom said we are supposed to share. Aaron, tell her to give me some tattoos!"

Me: more silence. More staring.

Andrea: "Mom, Aaron's not helping me! Tell him to help me!"

Mom and Dad: unaware, blissfully asleep upstairs.

I decided to eat some breakfast and wait for the sun to rise. At some point the argument concluded and Wesley decided to put some of her tattoos on me. I knew she was adhering them onto various parts of my body, but it didn't matter. They would wash off. At least that's what I assumed.

The next day I went back to my routine. At five o'clock I left my office, drove a few miles down the road, and parked my car at the gym. I greeted the lady at the front desk, changed my clothes in the locker room, and just as I was walking into the workout room, I noticed an enormous pink Easter bunny, holding a basketful of pastel Easter eggs, smiling at me from my left shoulder. It probably wouldn't have been so bad had I not then noticed his purple friend on my other shoulder. I decided I'd chosen the wrong day to wear a sleeveless workout shirt.

I made a beeline for the bathroom sink, assuming the word *temporary* actually meant something. It turns out "temporary" is a total farce as it pertains to water-based tattoos. After five minutes of intense scrubbing, my new pink and purple buddies were just as smiley and vibrant as ever. There was really nothing I could do. I sat in the locker room for a few more minutes, contemplating my next move.

Should I go home? Should I work out in the long-sleeve dress shirt I wore to work? Maybe I should take a pen and color over the bunnies?

I decided there was no good option. I'd work out and hopefully no one would notice my furry friends. I had read something about never showing fear if you are attacked by a bear, or other wild animals, so I walked into the weight room *confidently*. I figured the same tactic that worked on bears probably also applied to oversized, testosterone-filled men.

I stopped to grab a drink of water before I started my run. That's when it happened. Suddenly, with no warning, as if he had appeared from thin air, the largest, scariest, most intimidating guy who worked out in that gym was standing right behind me. I tried not to panic. I attempted to inch my way around his massive frame, but his neck alone could have blocked the entire path. I did my best not to make eye contact so as not to provoke his attention. It didn't work. The jig was up. I tried to step to the left, but the man-mountain was one step ahead of me. I made a pivot move and then a quick stutter step, but he shut that down with little effort. I decided to capitulate. As we stood there in a vortex of awkwardness, the guy said, "Hey, sweet bunnies, bro."

What could I say? I tried to scramble. I tried to deflect. I thought about implementing the third-grade fire drill—stop, drop, and roll. Nothing seemed to work. This guy was locked in and he wouldn't let it go.

That was the beginning of my first conversation with Ben. I was petrified. I kept saying, "Ok, well, I better go now." There was literally no way around him. It turned out that Ben was a professional football player from a challenging background and his greatest joy in life was his seven-year-old sister, who lived in another state. Ben said with a grin, "My sister *loves* fake tattoos!" Apparently my bunnies reminded him of his sister. Who knew?

I saw Ben at the gym almost every day for the next week. Our relationship developed quickly. We spoke about his childhood, family, sports, and a bunch of other stuff people don't usually talk about in the gym.

It wasn't long after Easter when Ben called to talk to me about a personal matter. He sounded serious, so we decided to meet at the gym early the next morning. The next day, sitting in the locker room, Ben said, "Aaron, I'm having girl problems."

"Ok, what's the problem?"

"Well, there's this girl, Tina—we are dating."

"Is that a problem?"

"Not really, but there's this other girl, Stephanie . . ."

I picked up on the problem pretty quickly.

That morning we sat in the locker room for several hours. We spoke about Tina and Stephanie—and a few other ladies—but we also spoke more about God's outrageous invitation to help us navigate every aspect of life.

For over six months, I didn't know a single person in the gym. I was content. I was happy to just show up, turn the music on, and tune out. But as I've said, so often God has something more. So often God has an opportunity, event, or adventure waiting for us amid our everyday routine. The question is, *Do we expect him to show up and provide an outrageous opportunity, or not?* And, perhaps even more importantly, *Are we awake and willing to act when the opportunity arises?*

For months I had seen Ben as the largest, scariest, most intimidating guy in the gym. He was the last person I thought I would befriend, but that was *my* plan—God had something more. That morning as we sat speaking in the gym locker room, Ben said, "Aaron, I want the outrageous life that Jesus offers!" And right there, he accepted Jesus's offer and began the outrageous adventure God had always hoped for him.

One of my favorite authors is a great-great-great-grandson of the famous Dublin brewer Arthur Guinness—his name is Os Guinness. An Oxford PhD and former freelance reporter for the

BBC, he once said, "Our problem is not that we aren't where we should be, but that we aren't what we should be where we are."[3] I think that was my problem in the gym—I wasn't necessarily in the wrong place, but perhaps I wasn't seeing the situation for everything that it could and should be. I don't think the situation needed to change. I don't think I needed to remove myself from the situation. But I do think I needed to approach the situation in a different way—from a different perspective.

Sometimes I wonder if Ben would have placed his faith in Jesus if I had kept my headphones on and hadn't been open to getting to know him better. Now, I can't be sure, but my guess is that God would have seen to it that he did. But the thing is, *I* would have missed out on the opportunity to play a role, and that's why I want to awake to the opportunities around me *every day*. Even if that means a few Easter bunnies show up along the way.

---

3. Os Guinness, *The Call: Finding and Fulfilling the Central Purpose of Your Life* (Nashville: Word, 1998).

7

THE FOG

IT ALL STARTED ONE DAY in Santiago, Chile, while I was eating an avocado sandwich at one in the morning. My friend David said, "Do you think it's possible to share Jesus with one billion people at the same time?"

David is a guy who loves to think outside the box, and he always challenges me to dream *big*, God-sized dreams. David grew up in Cleveland, Ohio, the lastborn of ten children. He went to college on a soccer scholarship and immediately entered corporate America upon graduation. But David was never the stereotypical corporate-type; I don't think he owns a pair of pants to this day, and throughout his years as the Chief Storyteller at Microsoft, his preferred mode of transportation was a 50cc scooter.

I first met David a few years after he had moved his family from Seattle, Washington—to Santiago, Chile. That would be at the least an interesting move for some people, but it was a radical transition for someone like David. After twenty-five years in corporate America, David seemed to be living the American dream—big house, great family, and a dream job at Microsoft. Everything seemed to be going according to plan until the day Jesus revealed himself to David and gave him a new plan. One Sunday, just like any other, David was sitting in church and the pastor was speaking about how Jesus "called" the original disciples to leave everything and radically follow him. David says he always thought of himself as a "sender, not a go-er," but on that particular Sunday, amid the hundreds of other people at church that day, the pastor looked right at David and said, "If Jesus asked you to leave everything, would you go?" David decided he would.

When the president of Microsoft heard David was leaving the company, he told David's boss to make a better counteroffer than whoever was attempting to recruit him. David's boss simply responded, "You don't understand who we are competing against!"

So, one night we were sitting around David's little dining room table in a suburb of Santiago called Maipú (literally pronounced "my poo," which obviously creates numerous entertaining sub-conversations like, "Hey, what are you doing?" "Not much, just sitting around in my poo."), eating avocado sandwiches, when David said, "Jesus totally changed my perspective on who I am and what I'm supposed to do—that's why I'm in Chile! When people see Jesus, he can move them in outrageous ways."

That was the night we decided to do *something* that would help the one billion people who would watch the upcoming World Cup to see Jesus more clearly. We didn't know what we should, could, or would do, but we committed that night to do *something.*

About six months prior to the start of the Fédération Internationale de Football Association (FIFA) World Cup, David and I decided we should create a short film that would help people to see Jesus clearly. Neither of us had ever made a film, but a friend of a friend knew a guy who connected us with GED Media, an extremely accomplished motion production and commercial media company based in Oklahoma City. GED Media is known for their commercial work for companies like John Deere, Chesapeake Energy, Sonic, the New York Yankees, and Chevrolet. They wouldn't want me to say it, but they're a big deal.

Our first phone meeting went something like this:

Aaron and David: "Hey, guys, this might sound outrageous, but we want to make a film that will impact one billion people."

GED Media: "Ok."

Aaron and David: "We said one *billion!*"

GED Media: "Yup, ok."

Aaron and David: "We didn't say *one thousand.*"

GED Media: "Yup, we got it!"

Aaron and David: "Well . . . ok . . . when can we start?"

It took over two months and multiple brainstorming sessions, but one day Andrew, the founder of GED Media, called me and said, "I've got it . . . we need to build a door!" I'll be honest; I was skeptical. Andrew said, "We could use a framed, freestanding door to take the audience on a journey through different countries and cultures—the door would become a portal to the world, and whenever we walked through the door, we would see a new picture of God's creation that would ultimately culminate with a clear picture of who Jesus is."

I don't think I could *see* what Andrew was talking about as clearly as he could, but we decided to go with it anyway. Film production started two weeks later. We wanted the film to present a global picture, so we scheduled to film on four continents, in five countries, in just under two months.

Our first stop was Dubai.

We flew all night, from the United States to London and then on to the United Arab Emirates. When we arrived, an Australian nongovernmental organization (NGO) worker met us at the airport. The man didn't have a background in film, but he knew Dubai and was willing to show us our options. The only warning he gave was that it's illegal to film in the United Arab Emirates (UAE) without a valid UAE production trade license, which you can only get if you are a citizen of UAE—*of course.* That would have been good information to have prior to flying over thirty hours and ten thousand miles. It was too late. We were committed. So we decided we would film outside of the city in the desert at first light the next morning. It was a risk, but if we were caught our Australian friend said imprisonment would be the worst thing that could happen.

The next morning the Australian picked us up in front of our hotel at three thirty. With an hour until sunrise, he drove us into the desert, dropped us off, and said he would return when we were finished filming. At that point there was no turning back. We said a short prayer, set up the door and the cameras, and then we sat in the sand, waiting for the sun to rise. Words cannot appropriately describe the backdrop that emerged as the sun rose over the arid plains of the Emirates that morning. Standing 2,717 feet tall, the Burj Khalifa (the tallest building in the world) gleamed as the fresh morning sun radiated off its shimmering metallic exterior. It wasn't flawless, but we managed to get the shot, deconstruct our door, pack our equipment, evade interaction with local authorities, and catch a flight out of Dubai, all by lunchtime.

Our next stop was Kathmandu, Nepal.

It turns out it's not always easy to convince airline employees in the Middle East that the gigantic box you want to take as check-in luggage is actually just a door. I wouldn't exactly call it a *bribe*, but somehow we got the door from UAE to Nepal.

We spent our first two days in Kathmandu, the capital city of Nepal, driving everywhere looking for the right place to film. Every time we asked a local if we could have permission to film in their area, they smiled and then shook their head no. It seemed to be a contradiction, but we didn't want to argue, so each time we simply moved on to a new location. By the end of the second day, we had been politely rejected everywhere we went. Each time the person smiled widely but still shook their head no. We found out later that in Nepal yes means no and no means yes, at least when it comes to head gestures.

We eventually decided to film in the middle of the Pashupatinath temple. Originally constructed in the fifteenth century, the Pashupatinath temple is one of the largest and most sacred temples in the Hindu faith. I'm not sure if it was good or bad, but it was interesting to watch people's reactions when we set up our door in the middle of their five-hundred-year-old sacred Hindu temple. Regardless, there was a lot of head shaking going on that day. We assumed they were affirming our work, but we decided not to stick around too long to find out.

After two months of filming on four different continents we arrived in Brazil to capture our final shots for our ten-minute production. Perhaps you saw the 2002 Brazilian crime drama *City of God*, featuring one of the most dangerous, poverty-stricken shantytowns, Cidade de Deus? For some reason we decided that would be a good location for our film as well.

Our final day of filming was in Rio de Janeiro. We had the entire day to capture the last ten seconds of the film on location at one of the most famous cultural icons in the country—the Christ the Redeemer statue. We chose Christ the Redeemer as our final shot because we wanted to leave the audience with a strong visual image of Jesus in addition to the spoken image we had depicted throughout the entire film.

Our flight back to the United States wasn't until nine at night, so we decided to spend the morning relaxing on the Copacabana before filming. After lunch we leisurely made our way toward Corcovado, the mountain on which Christ the Redeemer stands. It was the perfect ending to the outrageous adventure of making the film—blue skies, sunshine, and fluffy white clouds filled the sky.

We took a tram to the top of the mountain and then ascended the remaining two hundred and twenty steps to reach the base of the statue. We were excited to get the final shot and go home after two months on the road, but somewhere between the Copacabana and Corcovado everything changed. Jesus had left the building. Well, he might have been there, but no one could see him.

As we stood at the base of Christ the Redeemer, all we could see were the dark gray clouds that now swirled and engulfed the entire statue. We waited, but the weather only got worse. The clouds got thicker. The sky got darker. It quickly became obvious to everyone standing there: if you can't see Jesus, you might as well go home. And so most people did.

We were on that mountain for one reason—to see Jesus. We needed to get that final shot or we couldn't finish the film. We had no plan B. It was horrible. Jesus was so close, yet we couldn't see him. We waited one hour. Nothing changed. We waited two more hours. Nothing changed. After five hours almost every tourist had come and gone, and we decided we couldn't wait any longer or we would miss our flight home. As we were packing the camera equipment, one of the Brazilian cameramen said in broken English, "Hi, guy, we do pray together, Jesus?"

I was fairly certain he was suggesting we should pray. Actually, I'm not sure why I hadn't thought of that idea myself.

For months our small crew had flown to every corner of the globe to make a film about the power and presence of Jesus, but in that moment, literally sitting at the feet of Jesus, we forgot to look *to* Jesus, who is able to accomplish immeasurably more than we can on our own.

That afternoon my friend prayed one of the most earnest prayers I have ever heard. Huddled at the base of Christ the Redeemer, he prayed, "Jesus, we can't do our job if we can't see *you!*"

I've noticed we can't usually physically *see* Jesus like we hoped to see that statue standing atop Corcovado Mountain, but we can always look *to* him. In fact, Jesus has extended an invitation to each of us to experience an outrageous life, but it always begins, is sustained, and is made possible, by looking to Jesus alone.

As our small crew stood on the mountain, looking toward Jesus together, something outrageous happened—*Jesus revealed himself*. Some might say it was outrageous that we prayed and the clouds parted just long enough for us to capture the final shot of our film. We did, and that happened, so perhaps it was. But I think the outrageous thing was actually that we could see Jesus, who is always present and willing to make his power known whenever we look to him and ask.

Two months later, David and I launched our short film through the church in Brazil during the 2014 FIFA World Cup. We don't have one billion views *yet*, but when you are awake to the power of God made known when you look to Jesus, outrageous things will happen. Even if you happen to be sitting around in Maipú.

8

SHAG THE BALLS

SEVERAL YEARS AGO I was living in Cape Town, South Africa, playing soccer in their local league. Soccer is a big deal in South Africa. Baseball is not. Now, there may be a handful of people in South Africa who know what baseball is, but as far as most South Africans are concerned, there's really only one sport played with a bat—cricket. That's why I was surprised when five Major League Baseball players from the United States decided South Africa was the best place to share their knowledge of the game.

One day my phone rang and a friend said, "Hey, Aaron, what do you know about baseball?"

"My dad played baseball, that's about all I know. Why do you ask?"

"Well, there are some American baseball guys who want to visit South Africa, and they need someone to help coordinate their visit."

I didn't want to be a downer, but I replied, "You know South Africans don't play baseball, right?"

"Well, some do!"

Apparently my friend really wanted these guys to visit. Regardless, I made one more attempt to be the voice of reason. "Maybe you should tell them to go to the Dominican Republic, Cuba, or Japan?"

Unfazed, he replied, "Ok, maybe. But can you help?"

It didn't make sense to me, but the players wanted to visit South Africa to share the hope they found in Jesus. I thought to myself, *What's the worst thing that could happen?* I figured we could find a few baseball players somewhere, so I said, "I'm in."

A few days before the players arrived, I received an email that was titled, "The Itinerary." The players didn't intend to stay in Cape Town long, but they had some specific ideas about what they wanted to do and where they wanted to go. I was happy to accommodate them.

Now, I don't know much about baseball, but when I saw these players at Cape Town International Airport, I recognized them immediately. I saw one player who had won the Cy Young Award the year before. And another, who had retired, was an All-Star for many seasons. I'm sure if these guys walked down almost any street in America, a crowd would form. Autographs would be requested. People would shamelessly attempt to pose with them for selfies. But not in South Africa—no one else seemed to know them at all, and no one seemed to care.

The guys had only two days in Cape Town so we went from the airport directly into their itinerary. First stop, Cape Point.

Cape Point is the southernmost point in Africa, or so the experts say. In my opinion, there's nothing amazing about the point other than that it's where the Atlantic and Indian oceans meet. Regardless, millions of people visit Cape Point every year. My new baseball friends and I were no exception.

We arrived at Cape Point about midday, just in time for lunch. Everything was going according to the itinerary—that is, until the baboon showed up. Now, I'm not talking about one of those cute, cuddly monkeys you might have seen at the zoo. I'm talking about a real-life, fang-toothed, wild, bare-bummed *baboon*.

As we pulled into the parking lot, I turned the engine off and we opened the van doors to get out. That's when the screaming began. I was confused because it wasn't the type of yelling you might imagine manly, world-famous athletes would make. It was more like a scared troop of twelve-year-old Girl Scouts. It wasn't pretty. When we had opened the side door to get out, a baboon had jumped into the van—along with us! I jumped out of the front door, and in my panic my first thought was to make sure the doors were unlocked. I hit what I thought was the unlock button on my key remote. Unfortunately, I hit *lock* instead. I stood there for half a second, thinking, *This is crazy. Why aren't these guys getting out?* before I realized—*They can't get out!*

Finally, the guys fled from the van like criminals from the scene of a crime—followed only seconds later by the baboon, holding the large backpack filled with our lunch. Standing there on the roadside, each of us in a defensive posture, we watched the baboon saunter around the vehicle with our lunch in hand. And then, after a few laps around our car, it sat down on the pavement, opened the backpack, and proceeded to eat *everything* in the bag—literally. Only breaking occasionally to look up and laugh at us as he ate all our food.

Day one. It didn't quite go according to plan.

The itinerary for day two stated we would go into an under-privileged area of Cape Town to conduct a baseball clinic for disadvantaged youth. At breakfast I said, "Ok, so the plan is to find a few kids to play baseball with today, ok?" The guys seemed enthusiastic. One guy responded, "I think we can handle a few hundred kids, at least." Everyone seemed to agree. Everyone but me, that is.

I certainly wanted to help them achieve their goals for their trip, but I still wasn't convinced that we could find ten kids who play baseball in South Africa, let alone two hundred. So I said, "Ok, just so we're clear. What's your main objective for today?"

"We want to connect with kids through baseball so we can share the love of Jesus with them," they responded. I still wasn't convinced about the baseball part of the plan, but they felt certain it would work, so off we went.

We arrived in a disadvantaged area, referred to by locals as a township, about ten in the morning. It was a school day, but in many of those communities the parents aren't able to send their children to school. When we arrived, there were hundreds of children playing in the streets.

Within a few minutes we had about fifty kids congregated in an open field. As we attempted to organize the children, I noticed broken glass, rocks, and trash scattered everywhere. It wasn't the safest environment, but that's the field the kids always played in.

Once the kids were organized into semi-straight lines and sitting in the dirt, the Cy Young Award–winning pitcher stood up in front of the group. At six foot four, he towered over the children. They looked up in awe. Not necessarily because he was a famous baseball player, but just because he seemed really tall.

"Hello, everyone!" he said enthusiastically. "How many of you kids like to play baseball?"

No one said a word.

No one raised his or her hand.

After a few seconds of awkward silence, he said, "Ok, how many of you kids want to play baseball?"

Again, no one said a word.

No one raised his or her hand.

Finally, he said, "Do any of you know what baseball is?"

No one responded.

I sat on the side of the field as the baseball players huddled together to make a new plan. They decided instead of trying to explain the game, it would be best if the kids just played. Each kid got a glove and a ball and then watched as the players demonstrated how to throw and catch. "Now you try!" said the players. And immediately, every kid took off his glove, dropped the baseball to the ground, and used his foot to kick the ball to his partner. "Stop!" the baseball players shouted. "You are supposed to *throw* the ball to your partner!" To which one little boy responded, "But it's much more fun to kick it!"

The players decided it would be better to hit balls into the air and to have the kids in the outfield trying to catch them. The only problem was that when the kids were assembled in the outfield and a ball was hit into the air in their direction, they pretended the balls were atomic bombs and ran for cover.

The players seemed to be out of options, when one of them said, "Let's just play! Every kid loves to play, right?" Of course, the kids didn't know the rules, and they didn't know what to do, but the baseball guys divided them into teams and sent them out around the field standing in pairs.

Unfortunately, there were four kids too many, so the most famous player of the bunch got down on their level, on his hands and knees. He spoke in a very excited voice and said, "Kids, don't worry. Today you have the most important job!"

They stared back at the player, awaiting their assignment.

He said, "Kids, today you get to shag the balls!"

The kids just sat there.

They didn't move.

So, he said again, this time in an even more excited voice, "Come on, kids, this will be fun. You have such an important job; you get to shag the balls!"

By this point the kids, who were roughly twelve years old, had closed their eyes and were adamantly shaking their heads no.

Oblivious, the baseball guy made his statement one more time, but the kids simply refused to go.

I was still sitting on the sidelines when I overheard the conversation, and I ran over to assist. I could see that my new friend was perplexed by the kids' unwillingness to participate. He was definitely well-intentioned when he assigned the kids their jobs, but the problem is that in South Africa the word *shag* doesn't mean "collect," like it does in the States, and it's probably not advisable to casually use the word in public, especially not with kids. So when I whispered in his ear what I thought the kids were hearing, he immediately shouted, "Stop! No one shag anything!" That only seemed to exacerbate the situation, but at least he was now in the know.

We spent over two hours on the field that day, but oddly, no one ever played baseball. The amazing thing is when the baseball players realized their original plan would not work, they didn't force the issue. Instead, they put the equipment away, gathered the kids around in a circle, and just talked. The players shared about their lives in America and asked questions about the kids' lives in South Africa. Toward the end of the time, one player said, "Kids, we came to invite you to play baseball today, but Jesus has invited you to be part of something so much better." And right there sitting in the dirt, amid the broken glass and scattered trash, almost every child received Jesus's invitation to begin an outrageous life with him.

As I drove the players to the airport later that day, we all laughed about the baboon that stole our lunch and about how inappropriate the player's comment about shagging the balls was. That's when one guy said, "You know, nothing really went according to the itinerary we created for this trip, but it all worked out in the end."

I couldn't disagree. I've noticed that's often the case when God is involved. Although we love to create our own agenda, plans, schedules, and itineraries, God invites us to something more. That's why I've decided I want to awake to God's agenda and not be set in my own. It's difficult because we can't predict what God might do, or the opportunities he has in store, but if we are awake to his agenda and willing to lay down our own, outrageous things are often the result.

ANNUAL MEETING

THE DISCIPLES WERE ORDINARY MEN. But when they connected with Jesus, outrageous things began to happen. Sometimes they sat with politicians. Sometimes they testified before kings. On many occasions they spoke with the most influential religious leaders of their day.

Sometimes I wonder what these ordinary men felt like standing in front of large crowds of people or sharing the hope they found in Jesus with politicians, kings, and religious leaders. The day I met Papa G, I think I got a glimpse.

A few years after I met Jesus, a church in Nigeria invited me to Lagos to teach twenty guys from their church about how to coach soccer and share Jesus. At the time I wasn't really a coach; primarily I was still a player, but the church didn't seem to mind.

The invitation came from the personal assistant of a man named Papa G. I hadn't heard of him, but his title on the bottom of the very official block form letter was "General Overseer and Prophet of the World." Needless to say, I was impressed.

The letter began, "Dear Coach Aaron . . ."

I think I was twenty-two at the time, so I wasn't used to receiving official letters of invitation on company letterhead, or a cool title like "Coach."

The letter continued, "Please kindly consider coming to Lagos, Nigeria, to share your knowledge of soccer with our very eager ministers of the gospel serving in our soccer outreach program."

I was intrigued, but the most compelling part of the invitation was in the final paragraph, where it said, "Of course, our church, the Redeemed Christian Church of God, will cover all of your expenses." As a lowly paid twenty-two-year-old athlete, I felt the decision was a no-brainer. I thought, *Free food for an entire week!* No offense to my Nigerian friends, but if I had known what Nigerian food tasted like at the time, I probably wouldn't have gone. As they say, ignorance is bliss.

I arrived in Lagos at three in the afternoon. As I stepped off the plane into the sweltering midsummer heat and humidity, I wondered, *How will I find whoever it is that's supposed to pick me up?* I hadn't traveled alone much at that point in my life; so as hundreds of sweaty Nigerians pushed their way into the baggage claim area that was the size of a cereal box and simultaneously began shouting things like, "Don't touch that! That's my bag! Hello, hello, move, man!" I immediately felt my decision to visit Nigeria had been made too hastily.

I stood by the baggage claim carousel for over an hour, until everyone else had retrieved their luggage and gone. My bag never came. I walked up to a lady clipping her toenails at the counter marked "Customer Service."

"Hello," I said. "I have a problem. My bag never came."

The lady didn't look up from her pedicure. So I said again, this time a bit more assertively, "Hello there! I have a problem. My bag never came!"

As she lifted her head, I could almost hear her neck creaking like a rusty door slowly being opened.

She stopped her clipping just long enough to say, "What!" with an intimidating glare thrown in for free. I looked around to make sure I was in fact standing at the customer service counter. As best I could tell, I was. So, I said again, "My bag never came."

Now fully engaged in the conversation, the lady thought for a moment, shuffled some papers around the desk, and then shook her head back and forth as she replied, "Well, I guess it's lost then."

I eventually filed a claim for lost baggage, but I walked out of the airport with only the backpack carrying my then state-of-the-art laptop that weighed about twenty-five pounds and the old soccer jersey, khaki pants, and flip-flops I was wearing.

As I stood on the curb, the sun was beginning to fade into the horizon. Large Nigerian men wearing white flowing outfits similar to what my grandmother used to wear to bed were shuffling everywhere, shouting, "Taxi! Taxi! Taxi!" I was clueless as to what I should do, feeling overwhelmed and helpless. But then the limousine arrived.

The limo parked directly in front of me, and a man in a black three-piece suit rolled down the tinted backseat window halfway, leaned toward the door, and said, "You must be Coach Aaron. Please, get in."

I remember trying to organize a limo for my friends and our prom dates in the eleventh grade, but we couldn't come up with enough money. So this would be my first limo ride. I jumped into the backseat like a six-year-old at Disneyland, and we headed for the church.

"Hello, Coach. My name is Pastor Enoch from the Redeemed Christian Church of God. I will be your host."

Enoch spoke perfect English with a Nigerian twist. He was stately looking, and it wasn't just because he wore a three-piece suit. He seemed dignified.

I said, "Hello, Pastor Enoch. I'm sorry I'm not dressed appropriately, but the airline lost my bag." He seemed empathetic as he snapped his finger in the direction of the driver, who then lifted his eyes and peered at us in the rearview mirror. Enoch waved his right hand in a circular motion, pointed at me, and then said, "I'm so sorry, Coach. We'll have that taken care of."

By the time we arrived at a place Enoch called "the campground," the sun had set; it was completely dark. I was opening the limo door when Enoch abruptly put his hand on my shoulder and said, "Coach Aaron, are you ready? We will now see Papa G!"

I still didn't know who Papa G was, but his name alone intrigued me. As we walked into his ornate, plush red office, I thought, *This can't be one man's office; it looks like the Taj Mahal.*

There were seven or eight men in suits all standing in front of plush red-velvet chairs. No one spoke and no one sat down, so I stood too. After about ten minutes, my legs began to ache and I started to wonder, *What exactly is going on?* And then, all of a sudden, a door in the back of the room swung wide open and a miniature man who may have been a dwarf, or perhaps I should say "a person short of stature," walked out and announced, "Papa G shall enter the room!"

I would imagine that would have been the perfect moment for a few short trumpet blasts, but with no further formalities, Papa G walked in. To my surprise, all the men in their three-piece suits dropped to the floor. They lay on their stomachs with their arms out to their sides and their faces toward the ground. I had absolutely no idea what I should do.

So I just stood quietly as Papa G made his way around the room. I watched him walk up to each man, bend over, place his right hand on the back of each man's head, and then shout something in a foreign language as he shoved the man's face closer to the floor. When he finally came to me, I was thinking, *Should I sit? Should I keep standing? Should I dive to the ground like the other guys?* I didn't know. Somehow I ended up in a semi-kneeling pose, with my hand extended above my head. It felt like the time I did yoga and the instructor made me stand in the warrior pose, or maybe I was more like Sir Lancelot and Papa G was King Arthur, preparing to knight me for a battle.

I'm sure I didn't spend more than fifteen minutes with Papa G, but our brief chat was definitely helpful. As we spoke, different assistants would crawl—yes, I do mean *crawl*—on their hands and knees into the room, holding trays of food and drink. They would never make eye contact with Papa G or any of the other guests. And whenever they approached Papa G, it seemed important that they remain in a lower position than the golden chair he sat on. I think it was a throne.

As Papa G sipped his mango juice and ate several chocolate chip cookies the assistant called *biscuits*, he said, "Coach Aaron, do you know why I brought you to Nigeria?" Based on the two hours I had just experienced, I was starting to wonder why. So I didn't say anything, I just shook my head—*no*.

He said, "I oversee the Redeemed Christian Church of God and we have over fourteen thousand churches around the world." And then, after pausing briefly, he said, "We want more."

I just sat quietly, assuming it was the correct thing to do.

Papa G continued, "Our church has identified that people love the sport of soccer, and we believe the church can use that to share about Jesus's love."

I nodded my head—*yes*.

"We know you are a man of God who is skilled in soccer, so that's why we brought you here—to help us."

I don't think I had said a word when Papa G abruptly got up from his throne and appeared to be departing. All the men in suits immediately dropped back down to the floor. I remained seated.

As Papa G was walking away, he turned back to me and said, "Oh, yes, Coach, tonight is our annual meeting; I want you to speak about Jesus and soccer." And then he walked out the door.

When it was clear that Papa G had left the building, the men all began to talk. Enoch immediately ran over to me with a huge grin plastered across his face. He seemed *really* excited as he said, "Papa G must like you; he invited you to talk at our annual meeting!"

Now, it's important to note exactly who I was the night Papa G asked me to speak. I was a twenty-two-year-old soccer player from an ordinary family in the United States, and I had only spoken in public a handful of times. But that night, as I walked onto the open field where the Redeemed Christian Church of God held their annual meeting each year, I got a picture of what the disciples might have experienced at times and how they might have felt.

I've noticed that when you connect your life to Jesus it doesn't really matter where you are from, what you've done, what you can do, or what you happen to be wearing; Jesus is the X factor—he expands your influence in accordance with *his* outrageous plan.

That night in Lagos, Nigeria, I wasn't prepared or qualified to speak when I walked out onto that stage. And I probably wasn't dressed right either. But that night, Papa G stood up on the stage, invited me to stand with him, and then he said, "Come, Aaron, share with us."

So I shared my story of faith in front of the one million people sitting in the field that night—how I met Jesus in college and how he had totally changed my life. Of course, I was nervous. I was intimidated. I felt like I didn't know what to say. But as I shared, I felt the presence of God, who expanded my influence enough to allow me to speak at an annual meeting.

I've noticed when you are awake to influence not of your own, you never know when you might find yourself with kings, presidents, or prophets of the world named Papa G.

10

YOU DON'T HAVE TO DO THIS

SEVERAL HUNDRED YEARS AGO some deep thinkers met in Scotland to discuss their opinion on several theological issues, one being the chief end of man. A document called the Westminster Catechism was the result of these discussions. In it, those individuals state, "Man's chief end is to glorify God, and enjoy him forever." If that is true, the most important question becomes: What does this look like for *you*? What does it mean to glorify God, and how would you go about that if you decided that's what you wanted to do?

When I was growing up, my chief end was always *me*. It wasn't until I encountered Jesus my freshman year of college that I thought much about anything beyond myself. Perhaps that's why Singapore was such a revelation.

I went to Singapore for one reason—you guessed it—*me*. At the time, I had been playing professional soccer in Africa for several years. Professional soccer in Africa wasn't what I grew up dreaming *professional* soccer would be. I spent almost two years in Africa sleeping on the floor of a Baptist church, hitchhiking around the continent with anyone who would give me a ride, and generally just trying to create enough income to ensure that I could survive. That wasn't always easy.

Early on in my time in Africa, I arrived at practice one day and all of the players on my team were sitting outside the locker room in their street clothes. The captain of our team promptly said, "Aaron, don't change your clothes. We're on strike!"

On strike?

"Yes, everyone on the team agrees. We won't practice again until they pay us some of our salary, at least enough for bread."

As a kid I had thought being in professional sports meant being able to drive a fancy car or buy a huge house. I never dreamed it might mean wondering if you have enough money for bread. But that was our reality. We went on strike at least two times each month.

Now, I shouldn't complain, because I went to Africa of my own volition. I was a soccer player and I wanted to use soccer as a platform to make a difference in the world. I wanted to serve others. I wanted to share my faith. I wanted to glorify God. I just didn't realize exactly what that might mean.

So when I got an email out of the blue inviting me to visit Singapore with the possibility of playing soccer there, I remember thinking, *Who knows? Maybe it will be easier to glorify God in Singapore than it is in Africa.* So I went.

Singapore was like a dream to me. In a matter of hours I'd gone from flagging a ride on the side of a dusty African road to being picked up in a limousine in what is arguably one of the most modern cities in the world. This city that is also a country is filled with glass-paneled high-rise buildings, fancy cars, fast-talking people, and any amenity or convenience you might want. All of a sudden my world had radically changed; I no longer needed to hitchhike to practice, go on strike with my team when we didn't get paid, or sleep with cockroaches that would occasionally crawl across my face.

I believed I was finally in the place I was always meant to be. Growing up, I thought professional athletes were superheroes. They were able to do spectacular things on the field or court, and outside of the game they seemed to have everything going for them. Singapore felt like that to me.

Most mornings I would wake up on the thirty-fourth floor in my high-rise apartment, hang out at a swanky downtown coffee shop, read, pray, check email, and then take the bullet train to practice at a state-of-the-art facility. I felt a sense of achievement, validation, and justification for my years of hard work.

I had come to Singapore for the same reasons I had gone to Africa: to use soccer as a platform to make a difference in the world. I wanted to serve others. I wanted to share my faith. I wanted to glorify God. And the longer I stayed there, the more I believed it was just as possible to fulfill my purpose in Singapore as it was anywhere else.

One day I woke up and went through my normal morning routine, but when I arrived at practice, I experienced something different. On that particular day, as I was walking from the train toward the practice facility, it occurred to me that God had really blessed me. I had gone to Africa because I wanted to serve God and others. I had told God he could use my passion for soccer however he might desire. And now, though he was under no obligation, God had not only given me an amazing platform to influence others for his glory but had also given me many of the things I had always dreamed of.

I entered the locker room full of life. Or maybe I was just full of myself. That's a real possibility. In most every way it seemed like an ordinary day to me, but it wasn't. On that day, God had something more.

As usual, I greeted the other players as I walked through the locker room. I collected my training gear, changed my clothes, and then walked out the back door toward the practice field. The sun was shining and there wasn't a cloud in the sky as I walked onto the perfectly manicured grass field. I noticed a few guys laughing as they casually kicked a ball, a few coaches were standing near the center of the field talking, and a trainer was doing some rehab with an injured player off to the side.

That's when it happened.

I'm confident it had never happened before.

And actually, it has never happened again since.

I wasn't praying.

I wasn't singing worship hymns.

I wasn't even thinking about God at the time.

But as I was standing there in the sun, looking at the field, thinking about how perfect everything seemed to be—God spoke *to me.*

Aaron, you don't have to do this.

Since I wasn't praying, and the voice wasn't audible, I decided the voice I had heard couldn't have been God's. After all, I was standing on the soccer field, living my dream, about to practice—why would God be speaking to me?

That's when I heard the statement again.

You don't have to do this.

I thought to myself, *This can't be God!* So, again, I decided to ignore the voice. But a few seconds later I heard it again, this time a bit more pronounced. *AARON, YOU DON'T HAVE TO DO THIS.*

I don't know how you would respond if you thought you heard the voice of God, but I was actually annoyed. For twenty-something years I had worked, sacrificed, and even offered soccer to God. Now, all of a sudden, when I finally felt like I was living my dream, God was showing up with a different plan for me? I felt like he must have misspoken, or maybe he had the wrong guy. As I stood there, staring out at the field, my heart responded, *God, if this is you—what do you mean?*

As a freshman in college I came to know God and he started to change my vision for life, and many of my dreams. I stopped viewing myself as the sole chief end and started to care more about others' needs. The day I connected my life to Jesus, he began to shift my desire to more accurately reflect his heart for the world. The thing I didn't realize when I first came to know God is that Jesus doesn't just offer a new identity; he offers an entirely new purpose.

When God spoke to me that day, it was like the scales were instantly removed from my eyes, allowing me to see clearly that he wasn't talking about any soccer game but rather offering me an invitation to stop pursuing *me*. God was reminding me that my identity wasn't defined by what I have, who others said that I was, or what others thought of me, because I was not my own chief end. My purpose wasn't the pursuit of my own glory but rather *his* glory made known through me.

I can't tell you how long I stood on the side of field that day. But the one thing I know for sure was that all of a sudden, in that very moment, I knew I was free from any need to prove myself to God, others, and, especially, to myself.

I was filled with an immediate and overwhelming sense of release, and I instantly knew Singapore wasn't actually where I wanted to be. I walked directly up to the coach of the team, extended my hand, grabbed his, and as we shook, I said, "Coach, thanks for having me, but it's time for me to leave!" He may have responded, I don't know. I didn't wait to find out. I simply turned around and jogged off the field.

Six hours later I flew back to Africa. And while soccer is still a significant part of my life, it is not my god, my purpose, or my identity. It's a gift God has given me to enjoy and a tool I can use to give him glory, which is my chief end.

We're all here for the same purpose: to make known and reveal God's fame, renown, and significance above and beyond our own.

Now, I don't know about you, but I want to awake to how I can live for the glory of God. There's no greater aim.

11

IN A RELATIONSHIP

SEVERAL YEARS AGO I met a man while traveling on a bus through Africa. I had never met him before and I have never seen him since, but for twelve hours we shared a seat and our stories.

As we traveled the man told me about his childhood, his years at boarding school, his diamond business, and a favorite grandmother he loved to visit. We spoke nonstop the entire twelve-hour trip. Toward the end of our journey, this man I had never met concluded that I had a problem. He said, "Aaron, your problem is that you are single and you don't know how to fish." Apparently that was a bad combination.

The problem, he said, had to do with something his grandmother used to say: "If you want to catch a fish, you need to throw in your line."

I didn't have any evidence to prove the contrary, but I also couldn't agree.

———

As a single person, I always wanted to believe that God would provide the perfect life partner for me at the right time. It wasn't always easy. Especially once I turned thirty. Until then I hadn't thought much about getting married, but as the clock struck twelve on my thirtieth birthday, the internal questions began.

Will I ever find the right person?

Will I have kids? Will I be too old to have kids?

Is there one right person? How do I find that person?

Do I need to find that person? Will that person find me?

Am I too picky?

Everyone says she's nice, why don't I just marry her?

Sometimes the questions came from other people.

When do you plan on settling down?

Are you dating yet?

Have you tried Christian Mingle?

Being single simply isn't that easy. I often thought to myself, *Should I pray about finding a wife, or pray for my future wife?* But then I would immediately think, *Wait, what if I'm like the apostle Paul and God wants me to remain single?* I usually just ended up qualifying all my prayers with the all-encompassing blanket statement, *God, if it's your will . . .*

Almost halfway through my thirties, I was invited to spend six months in South Africa to help some churches facilitate outreach events around the 2010 FIFA World Cup. My primary role was to speak at these churches and at outreach events.

The first day I was in the country, I was asked to speak at four different events. It was a Sunday, and each event was held at a different church. By the time I arrived at the fourth church, it was already eight p.m., and while my spirit was willing my body didn't seem to share the enthusiasm.

I sat outside the sanctuary of the flagship Methodist church listening as a few thousand people sang songs of worship just beyond the doors. As I sat there, I prayed, *God, I need energy!* It was an honest prayer. I did need energy. The thing is, I just didn't realize how God would provide it.

A few minutes before I was supposed to speak, I entered from the back of the sanctuary and walked down the center aisle to my seat in the front. Now, I had spoken in many churches, in many different countries, but walking down the aisle of the church that night, I had an experience like no other experience I had ever had before. Somewhere between walking from the back to the front of the sanctuary, I was filled with a sudden and distinct surge of *energy*. Something like rocket fuel seemed to be injected into my spirit, and it immediately strengthened my body. In the moment, I didn't have time to think about it, but in hindsight it was obvious God answered the prayer I had uttered just moments before.

I stood in the foyer following the service and spoke with several people, as you do at events like that. I might have spoken with two or maybe even three hundred people following that service, but only one person stood out. I happen to remember everything about this particular person. We had never met, but now, many years later, I still remember seemingly insignificant details, like what she was wearing, where she had been sitting during the service, the bag she was holding, and her first words to me.

"Hello, my name is Ginny," she said.

Everything but her was a blur.

Ginny and I only spoke for about forty-five seconds. They were simultaneously the shortest and longest seconds of my entire life. She wore black knee-high boots, blue jeans, and a white sweater. She carried a black handbag and spoke with a beautiful English–South African accent. I wish I could remember what else she said that night, but I was preoccupied with trying to address a possible ethical dilemma—can a visiting American pastor ask a beautiful South African girl from the church he is speaking at on a date? It took the better part of those forty-five seconds to decide the answer. *No.*

That night, as I lay in bed in my friend's garage, a statement that my high school soccer coach loved to shout rang in my head: *Tredway, BIG mistake!* The interesting thing is that I never found that expression helpful in high school, and it wasn't helpful that night either.

I attempted to sleep, but I kept thinking about this South African girl I knew nothing about. *Is she married? Is she engaged? Where does she live? What does she do? Who is she?* I had no idea. I decided I needed to find out. As I lay awake, I contemplated calling the pastor of the church. But what would I say? "Hello, pastor, it's me, Aaron. I spoke at your church last night, and . . . I'm in love with the girl from the fourth row!"

I stayed in the bed the entire night, but I didn't sleep—not even for a second.

The next morning I got out of bed with the only hope I could think of—Facebook. I didn't know anything about Ginny aside from her first name, but as it turned out, that's all I needed to know.

Sitting in my friend's garage, I apprehensively typed: G-I-N-N-Y J-O-H-A-N-N-E-S-B-U-R-G.

And just like that, her face appeared in the blue-and-white-framed box!

Ginny Cooper.

It took me the next five hours to decide what I should say in a message to her. Even so, I won't lie; that first note wasn't a high point for me. I think "sister," "praying for you," and "God bless" appeared more than once. I decided it wasn't prudent to ask for her phone number or to suggest interest of any sort, but at least the note was a start. I wrote to Ginny Cooper. And even better, she wrote back—*immediately.*

I sat in front of my computer for several minutes before I opened her response and the accompanying Facebook friend request. When I finally did open her page, the first thing I noticed, in big bold letters, was: *in a relationship.*

I was crushed. *In a relationship*—it couldn't be! I reminded myself, *Well, at least your ethical dilemma is over, she's* in a relationship *so it's over before it ever could begin.*

Over the next month, I thought to myself on multiple occasions, *Maybe I read it wrong.* I often checked, but Ginny's relationship status never changed. The only thing I felt certain of was that she was definitely "in a relationship," and it wasn't with me. Regardless, we kept in touch. The first week we wrote once. The second week we wrote twice. By the end of the month we wrote almost every day, but nothing ever changed. Ginny was still "in a relationship," and I couldn't figure out with whom, or how serious it was.

For almost two months, Ginny and I communicated with each other only on Facebook. We never spoke on the phone or saw each other in person, but one day I realized my ethical dilemma had definitely returned. For all I knew, Ginny had always dreamed of having a pen pal from America. Perhaps she had no interest in anything but friendship. Maybe she simply wanted to ask me questions about theology and the weather, but the problem was, my intentions weren't the same.

Ironically, around that same time Ginny invited me to coffee, leaving me with only one choice. I said *no*. She then invited me to a soccer game; again, I said *no*. The following week she invited me to her birthday party. It was like some cruel single-man's torture tactic; perhaps, maybe, possibly, no, obviously I had to say—*no*!

The situation made no sense to me. I finally decided it couldn't continue. I promised myself that the next opportunity I had to end whatever it was that had begun, that's exactly what I would do. But I didn't. I thought to myself, *I'm sure I'll end this if I see her.*

The following week I was speaking in Cape Town and Ginny happened to be there. This was the time. This was the moment. I would definitely tell her this was the end of the road for us. We planned to meet for the first time since we'd met at her church at my speaking event that first night. Oddly, when we arrived, no one else was there.

How would you go about telling a girl (or boy) you could never speak with them again? When no one else showed up at the speaking event, *dinner* seemed a logical choice to me. Ginny and I drove in separate cars from the church to a restaurant in the center of town. As I drove, I rehearsed what I would say, but for some reason none of those things ever came out. We talked, laughed, ate, and did what normal people might do—*on a date*—but I knew it definitely had to be the last. That night we said good-bye. We didn't hug, kiss, or even high-five, but in the end we agreed that we'd see each other just one more time.

The next day Ginny and I climbed a mountain, drank some coffee, took a walk, sat by the ocean, ate dinner, drank more coffee, and by two in the morning, I finally decided, *This can't go on.* So, sitting in the lobby of her hotel, I knew it was time for me to go. I knew that once I walked out the door I would never see her again, so I decided that I might as well tell her exactly what I was feeling.

As I stood up to depart, I looked at Ginny, and when she looked back at me I said, "Ok, I'm leaving now, but you should know, I'm not happy with you at all!" Her only response was "Why?"

I thought it was obvious. I didn't feel I needed to explain the problem, but I expounded nonetheless. I said, "Well, I'm not happy because you are the most beautiful, intelligent, godly, and altogether amazing woman I have ever met, but you are already *in a relationship*, and that's a problem for me."

When I finished speaking, I was pretty pleased with myself. I thought it was at least a 9 out of 10 in terms of possible impact and dramatic affect. But Ginny seemed unmoved.

We sat in silence. No one moved. No one blinked. No one looked anywhere but the floor. And then Ginny called my bluff. She said, "Did I ever tell you that I was in a relationship?" I scrambled for a strong rebuttal, but I seemed to have used all my best stuff on my speech. The only thing I came up with was, "Um, no?"

"Well," she said. "Ask me, then."

"Ask you what?" I said, without a thought.

"Ask me, then, if I'm in a relationship. It seems like that's what you want to know."

So I said, somewhat flippantly, "Ok, then, are you *in a relationship*, Ginny from Johannesburg?" To which she simply responded, "No, I am not."

I don't know how long it took me to process that information, but sitting there in South Africa, on what may or may not have been date number two with a girl I had thought I could not date right up until that very moment, the only thing I could think to say was, "Well, for thirty-four years I have believed when you know . . . you just know. I think that we will get married!"

I suppose the more amazing thing is that Ginny responded, "That's what I think too!"

Perhaps the man on the bus in Africa was correct: you do need to throw in your line if you want to catch a fish. But I also know that Jesus has the power to choose the perfect fish, and allow her—or him—to jump right into your boat, in a totally unexpected, unconventional, and, perhaps you might say, *outrageous* sort of a way. I've noticed the way God often chooses to work in our lives isn't always the way we might imagine, but in the end it's always for our good.

I proposed to Ginny three months later in the middle of Hyde Park. It turns out even the angels of heaven were worried that I might never get married. The moment that Ginny said yes, several hundred members of the Vatican choir began rehearsing the Hallelujah chorus.

Ginny is from South Africa. I am from California. We live in Cleveland, Ohio. That might make us seem like an unconventional couple, but I think it makes total sense. We know an unconventional God who loves to give his children good gifts, often in totally unexpected ways.

12

BACKSIDE
PHILOSOPHY

I HAVE A FRIEND NAMED CHRIS. Chris is not
ordinary; there's something altogether different
about the guy. He doesn't tweet or post or blog
about what he does—he's too busy doing it. If I had
to bet, I'd go all in on Chris being a saint in street
clothes. He runs orphanages, looks after widows, cares
for the downtrodden, and doesn't think much about who may
or may not know.

Chris is from Zambia, but I met him in Timbuktu—not the
expression, the actual place. Timbuktu *is* the middle of nowhere,
located just north of the Niger River on the southern edge of the
Sahara desert in the West African nation of Mali. I met Chris on
a soccer field, where he was about to teach some kids how to
dribble the ball without stubbing their toes on the assortment of

rocks, trash, and debris scattered across the field that doubled as the village dump when it wasn't being used for soccer. Chris had a wide and infectious smile. I immediately noticed that he was commanding but gentle as he interacted with the kids.

I decided to introduce myself to him before the practice started. I walked onto the field past a grazing cow, what may have been a dog (though it could have been a rat), and a woman milking her goat. None of which seemed particularly bothered as I passed by.

I felt like the most conspicuous person in Timbuktu—I was likely the only *mazungu* [white man] within a five-hundred-mile radius. Chris noticed me immediately. We spoke briefly about what I was doing in Mali, and realizing my background in soccer, Chris invited me to play. Unfortunately I only had the clothes I'd been wearing since I left the United States three days prior. I had arrived in the middle of nowhere but my suitcase was somewhere else. Chris was unfazed. Within minutes I was wearing his t-shirt, shorts, and a pair of sandals with hanging leather tassels. I think he gave me his underwear too—but I chose to wear my own.

I ended up spending three days with Chris in Timbuktu. We became fast friends, which, I suppose, is only natural when you're wearing another man's clothes. When it was time to go, we agreed we'd hang out again somewhere closer to home.

That day came sooner than I expected. A few months later, Chris invited me to visit him in Zambia. He is a modest guy, so I didn't realize at the time we met that he leads one of the largest organizations in Zambia committed to sharing Jesus with others, an organization called Campus Crusade for Christ (CRU). When I received the invitation it seemed that Chris wanted me to help him with a grassroots soccer outreach program for kids. Upon my arrival in Zambia, I realized he had a much more elaborate plan.

Driving from the airport to the CRU office, Chris said, "What do you think about doing some coaching while you are here in Zambia?"

"No problem," I said. In hindsight, I should have clarified what type of coaching Chris was referring to.

The next morning he took me to meet with the Zambian Minister of Youth and Sport, the Head of the Olympic Committee, and also the president of the soccer federation. Of the three, I found the meeting with the soccer federation president the most interesting. As we sat in his office drinking overly sweetened tea and some type of fried, salty dough, he said, "So, Chris tells me you are an American coach?"

"Yes, I enjoy coaching very much." It all seemed very casual. Then, all of a sudden, the president said, "Congratulations, you are the new Zambia National Soccer Team assistant coach—effective immediately."

I figured that Chris had convinced his old soccer buddy to mess with me a bit, so I played along, but when we walked out of the president's office, I started to think, *Maybe they weren't joking.*

The next day I reported for duty at the National Training Center in Lusaka. My middle school soccer field was probably nicer than the Zambian National Training Center field, and it had half a baseball diamond in the middle. I walked in and introduced myself to the other coaches. I figured they would finally tell me this had all been a joke, but no one blinked an eye. The "kit man" gave me my training gear and showed me to the locker room, and then we headed for the field. It turns out Zambians don't joke about their national sport; six months later I was still the assistant coach of the Zambian National Soccer Team.

One day before practice I noticed a slight pain in my lower back. I decided not to mention it to anyone because it was actually my *extreme* lower back. I figured the pain would dissipate. It didn't. The next day the pain was worse, and over the next week it eventually became unbearable. I needed to get to the bottom of the situation, literally, so I called Chris. When I told Chris about the location of my pain, he took it upon himself to assist with a diagnosis. Casually poking around my lower quadrant, he determined I needed a doctor. (Apparently African people don't have the same spatial boundaries that we have in the West!)

Despite the pain, I didn't want to go to the doctor. I wasn't too enthusiastic about having a Zambian doctor poke around my lower quadrant and I didn't want to miss practice. I kept telling Chris, "I'm sure it's going to get better!" It didn't. Actually, it just got worse. I was frustrated because I was forming some great relationships with the players and staff and I didn't want to be away. But I had no option; I needed to find a solution. I couldn't walk. I couldn't even sit down.

Now, just in case you have never had a pain in your lower back, let me just say, sitting is not advisable if you need to drive to the doctor's office in a minivan along the softly paved roads of North America; it is a catastrophe if you're in Africa. I counted three hundred and eighty-seven potholes on the road from my guesthouse to the doctor's office. We didn't miss one. I was convinced that my taxi driver was hitting them on purpose. He did apologize each time, commenting repeatedly, "Coach—I'm sorry to hurt your bum!" He wasn't joking. I wasn't amused.

Chris took me to a private medical clinic. I think "private" and "medical" were probably optional traits. I noticed several people waiting in the lobby, but we seemed to bypass most of the formalities, as I was told Dr. T would see me shortly. Assuming whatever was about to go down might require some discretion, I asked Chris to wait in the lobby. He didn't seem to understand why I would want him to wait in the lobby, but he complied. Dr. T was a small, meticulous man, formally educated in London. He made no small talk upon entering the room but simply said, "Remove the pants." Apparently he didn't just mean my jeans. I'm not sure what standard practice for an examination of that nature might be, but I ended up kneeling on a wooden table wearing nothing but a t-shirt, dress socks, and shoes.

About thirty seconds into my table experience, I noticed an elderly gentleman standing in the doorway. He didn't look like a doctor—it turns out he wasn't. I guess patient privacy is discretionary in Zambia. It didn't take long for an enthusiastic crowd of onlookers to form. *Everyone* seemed excited to see the show. Dr. T didn't seem to notice. I felt like charging admission, or at least making some commission on the popcorn and candy sales.

It turned out that the source of my pain was easy to fix. The onlookers seemed disgruntled when I put my pants—and my pants—back on, like they hadn't received their money's worth. I was just happy the show was over.

I wanted to flee the scene as quickly as possible. I wanted to get back to my work with the national team. But Dr. T seemed like he wanted to chat. Initially I kept trying to expedite the conversation, to bring it to a close. Dr. T persisted. We talked about life in Zambia, his education in London, family, culture, and a host of other things. Two hours later, Dr. T said, "So, Aaron, why did you really come to Zambia if you hadn't planned on coaching the national team?"

The truth is, I was in Zambia because I wanted to share Jesus with those I might meet. For six months I had put all my focus and effort into building relationships with players and coaches, but in that moment, it occurred to me, *Maybe God wants to use me right here with Dr. T.*

I learned later that nurses scampered like squirrels collecting nuts for the winter when they heard me telling Dr. T about my faith in Jesus. Apparently those nurses had been praying for Dr. T to meet Jesus for many years, and that day God decided to answer their prayers, as Dr. T connected his life to Jesus right there in his makeshift operating room.

As I walked out of Dr. T's office, I thought to myself, *Maybe there was a reason for my pain.* I had thought the pain was simply a nuisance, something that took me away from my purpose, but I've noticed Jesus wants to make himself known and he's prepared to use a variety of situations to that end.

A few days later I was back to coaching, and Chris came to visit me at the field. As we spoke, he said, "Aaron, I've decided if Jesus can use your butt to make himself known, he can use just about anything!" I think Chris was right. So often we think that in order for God to use us to accomplish his outrageous purposes in the world, we need to have a certain job, education, talent, skills, ability, or other things. The truth is, God *does* use all of those good things, but he also uses what the apostle Paul called foolish things to accomplish his purposes. Paul talked about how God intentionally chooses to use things that other people think are weak, lowly, and ordinary so that when outrageous things happen, there's no question regarding who gets the credit. God alone!

So often we're ready and available to serve God in the situations and environments that *we* expect him to be in—church, Bible study, at work, or at school—but I've noticed that he loves to use unexpected situations too. He might also use something totally ridiculous, unexpected, and even outrageous—something like your butt. You just never know.

Now, I don't know about you, but I want to awake to God's use of foolish things to accomplish his outrageous purposes.

13

AMERICAN HAMBURGERS

MY FATHER-IN-LAW, Dave, is a real man's man. He likes beer, meat, and sports, mostly in that order. Dave is an engineer; he likes to build stuff. When he isn't building stuff, he likes to fix stuff. And when he isn't building stuff or fixing stuff, he's asleep. Ginny always says her dad only has two settings: on and off. There's nothing in between.

I first met Dave one winter day in South Africa. It was about forty degrees and he was wearing rugby shorts, a pair of Crocs, and absolutely nothing else. Dave grew up in England. I assume he owned a shirt. At age twenty-one he got offered a job in Johannesburg at a time when the South African currency, called the rand, was more than double the English pound. He took the job and he's never been "home" since.

Over the years, Dave has embraced many aspects of his new country, but the *braai* is the thing he likes best. Now, a braai is simply a barbeque. It's nothing more and nothing less. But to a South African the braai is not just a piece of equipment used for grilling meat—it's a rite of passage. It's something like a bar mitzvah for a Jewish boy or a quinceañera for a Hispanic girl, only without the ceremony. You either braai or you do not.

I must admit, when Ginny and I got married I didn't own a *braai*, but I did own a hair dryer, which probably wasn't considered a good thing in Dave's world since I don't drink beer and I happen to be a guy.

The day after Ginny and I got married, we moved to Cape Town and rented an apartment on the beach. We planned to stay there for a year, but somehow that year became three.

Just in case you haven't heard or seen or had the opportunity to visit for yourself, it's worth noting that Cape Town is the greatest city on earth. It has amazing beaches, forests, mountains, music, restaurants, and almost anything else you could imagine. The city even has its own slogan: "You don't need a holiday, you need Cape Town." So, within a few days of moving to our new city, Ginny and I felt we had almost everything we could need, but we still didn't own a braai, so in our first week of marriage, we went out and bought one.

We hosted Christmas at our house that December. Since Ginny is an only child there usually aren't many logistics to coordinate, but we all agreed that her parents would stay with us in Cape Town for just over a week. Now, as I grew up in California, Christmas to me never included snowball fights, sledding, or sitting around a wood-burning fire, but it also wasn't lying by the pool, walking on the beach, or wishing I had a fan either. Prior to that first Christmas in Cape Town, I had never internalized the fact that December in the southern hemisphere is summer, which means it's *hot*. Regardless, when sunburn is your greatest worry on a warm Christmas day, you don't qualify for complaining.

Christmas Eve morning we woke up early and decided to go for a drive up the coast. We stopped and had breakfast in a vineyard. We also had a coffee and went for a long walk near the sea. After a full morning of activity, it was time to go home, but first we stopped at the grocery store to buy food for dinner.

I'll be honest; I'm not usually the one who does the family cooking. In fact, before Ginny and I were married, our premarital counselors suggested that we should divide our family jobs. I thought it was a helpful exercise, although we now often joke that I took responsibility for the family fun and Ginny got everything else. Regardless, as we were walking through the store contemplating our dinner options, I said, "Hey, we should do barbeque hamburgers for dinner!" And there wasn't much debate. Everyone seemed to agree.

Sure, no one had ever had a barbequed hamburger aside from me, and it was noted that it seemed to be a very American thing to do, but still, *everyone* agreed—American hamburgers it would be.

A few hours later I was inside the house, sitting in my favorite chair reading a book, when Ginny walked into the room. I could tell there was a problem. I looked up from my book and said, "Hey, something wrong?"

She immediately responded, "It's *never* going to work!"

"What won't work?" I said.

"My dad says it won't work; it's impossible!"

I had no clue what Ginny was talking about.

"What won't work?" I said again.

"The *hamburgers*!"

Now very confused, I said, "Why, what's wrong with the hamburgers?"

"My dad says it's impossible to cook hamburgers on a braai!"

By that point I was starting to understand what was happening, but it didn't seem like the code red alert Ginny and her dad seemed to think it was.

"Why does your dad think you can't barbeque hamburgers?"

"He says they will all fall through the grate when you attempt to cook them. He says the only way to cook a hamburger is on a pan!"

I just smiled and said, "Oh, I see. Just leave this one with me."

I let some time pass before I made my way into the backyard and found Dave sitting by the pool. I casually approached my father-in-law of nine whole months and said, "Hey, Dave, Ginny told me we have a problem."

"Yes! I've been thinking about it, and you can't cook those hamburgers on the braai. It will never work!"

I remained completely nonchalant.

"Oh, really, what makes you think that?" I said.

"Well, for starters, I've never seen it done before."

I didn't think that really answered the question, so I inquired once more, "Why can't it work?"

He just said, "Trust me. It will never work! The hamburgers will fall through the grate!"

So, against my better judgment, I decided to let my naughty side prevail and I proposed a bet. I said, "Dave, I have to disagree with you. I think you *can* cook hamburgers on a braai." Of course, he disagreed. So, I said, "Ok, tonight I'm going to make the hamburgers. I'm going to light the fire, prepare the grill, and cook the hamburgers *on the braai*, without any help from you."

Now, standing a few feet from my father-in-law, I said, "And if those hamburgers *do* fall through the grate, you have my permission . . ." and I took my finger and pressed it on his nose, "to say to me . . ." I flicked his nose, "*I told you so!* But," I said, "if the hamburgers do *not* fall through the grate, and they are the very best hamburgers you have ever tasted, I am going to tell you . . ." I flicked his nose again. "*I told you so!*"

I suppose that proposal could have elicited a few different reactions, but after Dave had stared me down for a second, we both laughed and shook on the deal.

That night, I did everything just as I had proposed—I lit the fire, prepared the grill, and then cooked the hamburgers on the braai. For a brief second I thought to myself, *Are these hamburgers going to fall through the grate? Maybe this isn't going to work.* But it did.

I've noticed that I often approach God the same way my father-in-law approached me that afternoon. I question his ability. Of course, barbequing a hamburger is a *very* small feat, but maybe some of the things we think are impossible aren't such a big deal to God either?

So often when we haven't seen something done before, we haven't experienced it ourselves, or we don't know how to make something happen, we think it's not possible. But I've noticed when God is involved, anything can happen. It's not always easy to remember in the moment, but when you step back from any situation you might just realize that to God it's just like barbequing a hamburger—how difficult can it actually be?

14

PLAYING BEHIND THE DUMP

WHEN WE WERE GROWING UP, my friend Peter and I loved to play in the dirt. Most afternoons we could be found in the large dirt pit beside his house, burying time capsules, attempting to dig to China, performing geological excavation, or mud wrestling if it happened to rain that day. But of all the things we did in the dirt, our favorite activity was definitely playing *war*.

War was a game involving mud castles, bunkers, and green plastic army men. The game wasn't complex. We would each spend several hours creating an elaborate mud fortress to house our strategically placed army figures. At the given signal, each man would proceed to hurl premade mud balls at the opposition until all the army men were knocked down. That usually took about ten seconds. The process would then start over.

As much as I liked to *play* war growing up, I've never actually been in a war, but my friend Ishmael has. Ishmael didn't volunteer to participate—the war came to him. Ishmael grew up in Freetown, Sierra Leone, where a civil war began on March 23, 1991. Ishmael was seven years old.

War is devastating no matter what side you are on. Perhaps there were good reasons to fight, but none seemed worthy to Ishmael and his family. Although they never chose a side, the war still chose them. It lasted almost eleven years and spanned the entire landscape of the nation. When the civil war ended on January 18, 2002, Ishmael's family had lost their father, brother, two uncles, and six cousins, none of whom had signed up to participate in the war. No family remained untouched; over fifty thousand people from Sierra Leone were lost.

While the war brought devastation and loss to countless families in Sierra Leone, it also brought new beginnings. Ishmael, his mother, and his younger sister moved to the United States as political refugees in January 2001. Ishmael was seventeen years old.

I first met Ishmael in a small indoor sports complex in Cleveland, Ohio. In January. It was cold that day, the type of cold that freezes your eyelashes or your car door shut. It was well below freezing and near whiteout conditions, but Ishmael arrived wearing a T-shirt and shorts. I don't think he had many options. I asked him if he had any soccer cleats. He didn't say anything, he just shook his head—*no*.

When I met him, Ishmael didn't talk much but he ran like the wind. While growing up, he and his friends couldn't always make it to school but they always found a way to play soccer; you might say they *lived* for soccer. They could often hear guns being fired, the terrifying shrieks and wailing of injured people, and grenades being detonated in the streets surrounding them, but the boys still played. They had to play. Soccer wasn't just a game for these boys; it was their refuge.

Every afternoon Ishmael would sneak out of his one-bedroom house, occupied by ten family members who all slept on the floor, and run as fast as he could past the United Nations outpost on the corner of his street. When he would arrive at the major intersection, he would stop and look in both directions for cars, just as his mother taught him. At times, a large tank or hummer would drive past. He also kept an eye out for the bullets that routinely flew through the streets without any warning.

After running a few miles Ishmael would arrive at the city dump, where he and his friends played soccer each day. They didn't play in the dump, but they did play behind it. The dump was a safe haven, a place the boys could feel normal even if it was only for one hour each day. There were no guns, no rebels, and no fighting at the dump; there was also no grass, just a group of boys playing in the dirt.

The boys didn't have fancy uniforms or socks or the latest soccer cleats. Most of them didn't even have shoes, but they had hope. Most days, after they had finished playing, Ishmael and his friends would lie down in the dirt behind the dump and, as the day turned to dusk, they would dream together. Ishmael would often say, "One day, I'm going to play soccer in a real stadium with grass. There will be lights and people, and no one will be fighting anymore." Nothing in his life suggested that dream would ever be possible, but the thing is, you never know what God has planned.

Ishmael came to Cleveland because he had heard about a new professional soccer team, the Cleveland City Stars. He had never played professional soccer, but he had always been the best of the boys playing behind the dump.

The day I met Ishmael it was obvious that he was a gifted soccer player, but he was raw and unrefined. Perhaps he was raw because he had never had a coach, or maybe it was because he had never played with a ball.

While the only thing you *need* to play soccer is a ball, a ball isn't easy to find in a war zone. Ishmael and his friends never had a real ball, but the dump had plenty of trash, so they would make a ball from the trash and that's what they played with—a big ball of trash. The trash ball wasn't great. It didn't bounce. It wasn't solid. It would sometimes self-combust. But it served its purpose.

Over the years Ishmael and his friends made their homemade soccer balls out of numerous materials, but nothing compared to the condom. When the government in Sierra Leone started distributing condoms to combat the rampant HIV/AIDS epidemic, Ishmael was too young to understand the meaning of "safe sex." He had another use for the condoms. He saw the potential for them to be transformed into something he had always dreamed of having: a rubber soccer ball like he saw on TV. As it turns out, when enough eight-year-old boys pool their government-issued condoms, they can make a pretty awesome rubber ball.

Ishmael signed a professional soccer contract with the Cleveland City Stars in 2007, and he quickly became a local fan favorite. In 2008 he scored the game-winning goal in the Division II

National Championship game against Charlotte. He was an All-League selection that year.

Every country in the world has a national team for soccer. Sierra Leone is no exception, and the country invited Ishmael, who was now a green-card holder and permanent resident of the United States, to represent Sierra Leone in soccer.

Ishmael asked me to accompany him to Sierra Leone to witness this monumental event in his life. I was humbled and thrilled to participate. A few weeks later we traveled from Cleveland to Washington, DC, to Senegal, to Freetown, Sierra Leone. When we arrived there were reporters, cameras, and people everywhere. Ishmael had left his nation a refugee; he returned a hero.

The day before I was scheduled to return to the United States, Ishmael decided we should visit the place where his dream of playing soccer began—the city dump. He hadn't visited the dump in almost a decade, and while the war was over, the dump still remained.

We arrived around ten in the morning. There were a surprising number of people *everywhere*. People began shouting for Ishmael. People were praising Ishmael. Some were even singing songs about him. As we walked through the dump, people hovered around Ishmael like a swarm of bumblebees. Finally, we rounded a corner and that's when we saw them—kids of all ages, *playing behind the dump*.

The dump was just as Ishmael had described it. No grass. No lines. No referees. But there were some very talented kids. I noticed one immediately. I'm not sure what caught my attention. Maybe it was the fact that he scored a goal every time he touched the ball, or that he was built like a thoroughbred racehorse with a giant black afro. Whatever it was, I definitely wanted to know more.

After the game I approached this young man and said, "Hey, I'm Aaron, who are you?"

He confidently responded, "I'm called Bang-Bang!"

"Your name is Bang-Bang? Why do they call you that?"

"Because I bang in the goals," he said with a smile.

I quickly decided this was no ordinary kid. I needed to know his story.

"So, what do you do, Bang-Bang?" I asked.

"I play soccer," he said.

"Oh, who do you play for?" I responded.

"I play right here, behind the dump!"

I suppose I should have known.

I decided to spend the afternoon with my new friend Bang-Bang. His real name was Teteh Bangura. Teteh was eighteen years old. He grew up in Freetown and survived the war with his family. Although they didn't have much, the family had each other and a strong Islamic tradition. As we walked through the streets of Freetown, Teteh told me he always believed that God had good plans for him. I agreed.

That afternoon Teteh and I spoke about many things—life, our hopes and dreams, and God, who has good plans for our lives even when our circumstances seem bad. We had been talking for several hours when I finally said, "Bang-Bang, would you like to play professional soccer?"

He responded, "*Yes*, coach!"

I said, "Bang-Bang, would you like to come to Cleveland, Ohio?"

He said, "Yes, coach . . . where is that?"

I didn't intend to bring an eighteen-year-old kid home with me in my suitcase, but I do think God had a plan. That afternoon I reached into my backpack and pulled out a Cleveland City Stars T-shirt. I gave Teteh the shirt and draped a Cleveland City Stars scarf around his neck. It probably wouldn't hold up in a court of law, but I picked up a crumpled Kentucky Fried Chicken napkin that I found on the side of the road and wrote: "I, Teteh Bangura, agree to play soccer for the Cleveland City Stars."

At the bottom of the napkin I drew two lines and we both signed our names.

A few months later Ishmael was offered a great contract to play for the professional soccer team in North Carolina. Bang-Bang came to Cleveland. He didn't experience immediate success on the field like Ishmael had, but he did experience an outrageous God who brought him out from behind a dump in Freetown, Sierra Leone, where he was taught to follow Allah, to Cleveland, Ohio, where he met Jesus and decided to place his faith in him.

Years ago, when Ishmael would lie in the dirt behind the dump with his friends, listening to the sounds of war, the situation seemed bleak and hopeless, but he believed there was something more. It would have been hard to predict that this little boy from behind the dump would move to the United States, play professional soccer, and become a national star. It would have also been difficult to think that God would eventually lead him back to the dump, where he would meet another little boy and have the chance to be used to offer that boy the opportunity to live his seemingly impossible dream.

Life doesn't always make sense, but God has good plans for us, even amid the most challenging circumstances.

Ishmael now resides in North Carolina, having recently retired from professional soccer after a long and successful career. Teteh is now the captain of the Sierra Leone National Team. He is also one of the highest paid players from Sierra Leone anywhere in the world.

My friends Ishmael and Teteh inspire me to awake to the good plans God has for us, regardless of our circumstances. Because you never know when playing behind the dump just might be God's best plan for you.

15

T-NBA

WHEN I WAS A KID, I loved to play basketball with my best friend, Eric. We spent most afternoons shooting jump shots in his front yard and arguing over who was Michael Jordan and who was Scottie Pippen. I'm not sure what a half-Japanese Jordan might look like, but it probably isn't me.

By the eighth grade Eric and I were both almost six foot tall and wore size twelve shoes. I can't speak for Eric, but the eighth grade was definitely the pinnacle of my basketball career. We dominated, at least in our own minds. Who knows what might have happened if we had both kept playing, but seeing as there weren't many half-Japanese professional basketball players, I decided to focus my efforts elsewhere. I hung up my MJs at age thirteen.

A few years ago a friend of mine was in Tajikistan, working with the underground church, when he met the general of the Tajikistan National Army. At the time, I didn't know Tajikistan even existed. It is a mountainous, landlocked country in Central Asia with a population of roughly eight million people. Apparently the general of the army loved two things—vodka and soccer. I don't know much about vodka, but given my background in soccer, my friend asked if I would come to Tajikistan to meet the general and see what God might do.

Now, I've been on several interesting flights, but the flight to Dushanbe, the capital of Tajikistan, was definitely different. There weren't many people on the plane, but there were several birds. Really. There were actual *birds* sitting in almost every seat on the airplane. These birds weren't normal. Each of them was at least four foot tall and sat straight up, never moving from their assigned seats. I know they were birds because they had feathers and beaks and talons and wings, but the crazy thing is that they also wore helmets and shields and had swords attached to their backs. Oddly, none of the other passengers seemed too alarmed by the fact that we were sharing our space on the plane with the fighting birds, so I just sat quietly, hoping not to provoke them—the birds, that is.

I arrived in Tajikistan at eight in the morning. A large Russian-looking man named Boris, my friend's co-worker, picked me up from the airport. I figured we would go directly to see my friend, and perhaps the general. Boris had a different plan.

Boris drove me to every noteworthy sight in the capital. Every so often he would say, "We go!" And he would drag me out of the car, saying, "Take good photo here," in his deep, Russian-sounding voice. After several hours, we ended up in a musty gymnasium with what I can only assume were the ten largest men in Dushanbe. Boris was six foot ten, but he didn't mention until we arrived at the gym that he was the captain of the most popular professional basketball team in the country. The team played in the T-NBA—the Tajikistan National Basketball Association.

Now, the T-NBA isn't quite the NBA, but there were some good players at the gym. There were also some players who probably wouldn't have made my eighth grade basketball team.

Boris and I greeted each player with a firm handshake. Every time we met another player he would say, "Da, this is *the new American player*, Aaron." I didn't think much of it at the time.

A few minutes later, Boris called all the players to center court. I stood quietly among the giants as Boris spoke in Russian, motioning in my direction on several occasions. Each time he would motion my way, I would smile and nod my head in an affirming manner, like I knew what he was saying. When Boris finished speaking, there were some fist pumps and a few high fives. I dished out a few high fives as well. But perhaps I should have asked what we were celebrating first.

I met my friend that evening. As we ate dinner we spoke about the work he was doing with the underground church, the challenges of trying to facilitate that work in a predominately Muslim country, and how further establishing relationships with key government officials like the army general we planned to meet on Sunday would help their credibility and potential to continue the work. At one point my friend said, "Hey, I didn't realize you are so good at basketball." To which I responded, "Yeah, I haven't played for a while." He didn't say much more and he didn't make a big deal about it, so I didn't either.

The next day was Saturday, and there was a knock on the door of my friend's house around nine. Moments later Boris ducked his oversized body through the entryway and lumbered into the kitchen, where my friend and I were finishing up breakfast. He looked like Gulliver standing amongst the Lilliputians.

"Good morning, everyone!"

"Hello, Boris, how are you?"

He grinned, as much as a stoic Russian man might do. Then he said, "I'm excited about our game today!"

Since the big meeting with the general wasn't until Sunday, the plan, as I understood it, was to go watch Boris play basketball and then meet some of his friends afterward for dinner. I was happy to go along for the ride. That is until we arrived at the basketball arena and I was told that the president of the team wanted to meet with me.

Boris and I walked through a dark hallway and into a small room that looked to have been furnished during the Cold War. The team president didn't speak much English, but he said, "Sit, sit. We are happy." We sat together sipping black tea and eating the unleavened bread I was quickly becoming familiar with.

After a few minutes a woman came into the room, holding a multiple-page document entirely in Russian. Boris whispered in my ear, "This is your contract." I had no idea what he was talking about.

"My contract for what?"

"To play basketball for our team, of course!"

"I can't play professional basketball. I'm a soccer player!"

Boris looked confused. He sat quietly for a moment and then said, "You're American; everyone is good basketball player in America!"

I tried to explain that I was totally unqualified. That I hadn't played basketball since the eighth grade. Boris didn't seem to mind. He said, "We've already told the media. There are many reporters and people coming today to see the first American basketball player in the T-NBA."

I kept thinking to myself, *This is a really bad idea. Say no. Nothing good can come from playing in a professional basketball game, especially since you haven't played basketball in almost twenty years!*

Boris interrupted this internal dialogue when he said, "The army general is even coming to see you play. It's a very important game."

I felt unqualified, unprepared, and unable to participate, but I've noticed that God often chooses the unqualified to accomplish his work, so after a few more seconds of silent contemplation I said, "Ok!"

It turns out the T-NBA is more popular than I had thought. As the game was about to begin, several thousand people filed into the arena.

As I walked onto the court wearing my white, knee-length baggy basketball shorts with the green racing stripe down the side and a matching mesh tank top two sizes too big for me, I thought to myself, *Ok, this won't be so bad. I'll warm up with the team, wave to the crowd, and then take my place on the bench and watch the game. How bad could it be?*

Actually, I was having fun with the whole experience, right up until the whistle blew and the game began. That's when the team huddled together, the coach gave an impassioned pre-game speech in Russian, and then literally pushed me onto the court. The crowd was chanting and stomping their feet on the steel bleachers. I'm sure I looked bewildered as Boris shouted over the noise of the crowd and said, "Aaron, you guard him!" while pointing at the biggest, hairiest player on the opposing team. The man looked like the love child of Rocky Balboa's Russian nemesis Ivan Drago and Miss Piggy from the Muppets. (No offense meant to Miss Piggy.)

I thought about telling the coach that I couldn't play. But it was too late. The game had begun. I was either going to commit to the cause or be left behind.

The first few minutes of the game felt like I was running through a battlefield full of land mines and hand grenades. The man I was guarding happened to be the captain of the Tajikistan Olympic basketball team. He was almost seven foot tall and there was little distinction between the amount of hair on his head and the hair on his back. No more than thirty seconds into the game, he was already so covered in sweat that anytime I had to touch him it brought back memories of the Slip 'n' Slide I had when I was eight.

Over the next forty-eight minutes the opposition passed the ball to the man I was guarding ninety-nine percent of the time. He slam-dunked the ball directly over me four times and scored thirty-four points total. Our team lost—*badly*.

I walked off the court embarrassed and dejected. *Why did I allow myself to participate in something I am so clearly unqualified for? Why didn't I just say no?* I felt like hiding under a rock. But as it turns out, you don't always need to win the game to achieve success.

As I walked out of the basketball arena, my church-planter friend was standing with the army general. I was prepared to offer a lengthy explanation for my performance, but when I approached him he put his hand on my shoulder, smiled, and said, "You are a good basketball player. Our team captain usually scores fifty points!" Apparently the general was pleased, not because I was such a great player but because I had participated, something no American had done before.

———

I don't think my basketball skill made much of a difference, but my participation did. In our meeting the next day, the general said, "It's so good to create relationships through sports." And his receptivity to sports diplomacy opened a door that allowed me to bring an entire team of American professional soccer players to Tajikistan the following year. Traditional missionaries were being shut out, kicked out, and denied any access to Tajikistan, but because of the relationships God enabled us to form, the Tajikistan government hosted our group of Jesus-loving soccer players. We went to Tajikistan to play soccer but ultimately we proclaimed Jesus's outrageous love to the entire nation.

As it turned out, I also got paid to play in that basketball game. The payment? One live goat. Apparently that made me one of the highest paid players in the league! And one of the most popular too. I invited the entire team for a goat barbeque that night.

I've noticed it's not always our ability that makes the difference; sometimes it's just our willingness to try. So I've decided I want to awake to God's choice of the unqualified to accomplish his work.

16

SLEEP IN THE MIDDLE

WHEN THE SUN SETS IN AFRICA, it's dark—
really dark. At night in the remote villages you don't
watch TV, play on your tablet, or FaceTime your
friends. You talk or sleep. Some people talk in their
sleep. Regardless, the options are limited.

It was never my dream to go to Africa, but one day, out of
the blue, I received a phone call from a man I didn't know. He
was looking for a goalkeeper to travel with his soccer team to
Zimbabwe for three weeks. He said it was a mission trip. At that
time I didn't even know what a mission trip was. He told me that
the purpose of the trip was to connect with people in Zimbabwe
through soccer and to tell others about Jesus. That seemed like a

good thing to do, but it also seemed like an uncomfortable thing to do. I had just started my soccer career. I liked my apartment. I liked my car. I liked my girlfriend. And I liked my life in the United States, just as it was.

As the conversation concluded, I thanked the man for calling and politely declined his invitation. In response, he said, "Just pray about the trip. Maybe God has a purpose; maybe he wants to move you outside your comfort zone." I was fairly certain he did not.

I prayed for the next few weeks, but it wasn't about the trip to Africa. I couldn't stop thinking about Africa, and even though I wasn't praying about it, I still felt a strange urge to go. I started to think, *Maybe God is challenging me to step out of my comfort zone? Maybe Africa isn't so scary? Maybe I should go?* I didn't have a compelling reason why I should *not* go, so one day I decided—*I'm in!*

Two weeks later I was on a flight from San Francisco, California, heading for Harare, Zimbabwe.

Everything was brand-new to me that first trip to Africa. The sights, sounds, and smells—everything was different. There were people everywhere: vendors cooking corn over open fires and selling it to old men with no teeth, little kids with no shoes playing soccer, stopping reluctantly to allow cars to pass by, and hundreds of taxi drivers obnoxiously calling out, whistling, and gesturing to find their next customer. Africa seemed alive.

Our team was based predominately in the capital city, Harare, but one day we drove eight hours into the bush to a remote village few outsiders ever visited. The village had no running water. No electricity. No toilets—and almost no connection with anything outside their own community.

I had seen conditions like those in the village on *National Geographic* but never in person. As we drove in, I thought, *How do people live like this? How do they survive?* I leaned over to my friend Carlos and whispered, "Where do they all sleep?" I had no clue. Carlos didn't know either.

That afternoon we attended a church service held outside. Everyone sat under a tree. There was no microphone, sound system, PowerPoint, or DVD. Someone led us in singing a few songs, but there was no band, instruments, or written lyrics to help us sing along.

When the church service ended, our team changed clothes and walked onto a rocky patch of undulating dirt. Our coach seemed excited as he called us over and said, "Hey, guys, watch what happens now." He placed a single leather soccer ball on the ground. We had made no announcement. There had been no marketing, promotion, or advertising on our part, but within literally a few minutes several hundred children were on that field, running, screaming, kicking each other, and having the time of their lives.

For most of the rest of the day, as I stood on the side of the field watching those kids play, I kept thinking, *It's outrageous that God would choose to use a few white guys and a soccer ball to impact several hundred African children playing in the dirt with no shoes.*

The plan was to stay in the village that night and then drive back to the city the next day. So, as the sun was setting, our team divided into pairs and went to stay with the village families we had been assigned to. Walking through the village toward our assigned mud hut with my partner, Carlos, I thought, *It's not California, but it's only for one night.*

Carlos and I arrived at the hut, and as we entered we quickly noticed the heat. It was summertime, and of course, there was no AC, but I assume the temperature in the hut was made warmer because Mom, Dad, Grandma, Grandpa, a goat, and seven kids all lived together inside.

Mud huts are much more spacious than you might think. Our host's hut had two bedrooms and a common living area. But still, I didn't understand where so many people would sleep.

We had already eaten dinner when we arrived at the hut, but the family insisted we eat again. The mom kept saying, "I'm preparing fish, just wait, we are all going to eat together!" It was roughly one in the morning when all the food was finally ready and the family gathered to pray. "Oh, God, thank you for providing for our needs today," the dad stood and prayed. And then, all at once, everyone said, "Amen!"

About three a.m. the party seemed to be winding down, so I excused myself to change. When I returned I found that Carlos had claimed a spot on the floor to sleep with all the kids. I wasn't exactly sure why, but he said I could have the bedroom. I didn't give it much thought. As I climbed into the bed and quickly dozed off, I remember thinking, *Carlos is such a good friend.*

All of a sudden, I woke up with the distinct sense that someone was standing over me. I was afraid. It was really dark, so I couldn't see who it might be. *What do I do? Should I yell? Should I fight? Should I just lie here and hope they go away?* I chose the least aggressive option. I just lay there, pretending I was still asleep. But then, without so much as a hello, the four-hundred-pound African mama bulldozed her way into bed. Yep—*with me.* So there we were. Both tucked in, under the covers. Lying side-by-side, together, the mom of the hut . . . and me.

I lay there thinking, *What can I do? What should I do? Maybe I should say something to her? Wait, she's starting to snore.* I quickly realized that Mama wasn't interested in anything but sleeping. I won't lie—I was relieved. We were sharing a double bed; she occupied at least eighty percent of the space, and her body mass had me pinned against the wall. It was awkward. With only three or four more hours left in the night, I decided I would just try to go back to sleep. But I was abruptly awakened again, with the exact same feeling I had before. I was afraid. I wanted to scream, "Help! I'm trapped!" But that's when I realized it was the dad of the house, who promptly climbed into the bed on my other side.

I lay there contemplating a million reasons as to how and why I had ended up in a mud hut, in a double bed, sleeping in the middle of a married African couple. I thought, *Maybe God is punishing me. Maybe I shouldn't have come to Africa. Or maybe this is a test. Maybe God wants to see if I'll just lie here or if I'm willing to take a stand and flee.* I decided I needed an exit strategy.

Now, you would think it would be simple. *Just get out of the bed!* But I assure you, there was no simple solution.

Picture this: Mama is on the outside of the bed, still occupying at least eighty percent of the space. Dad is against the wall. I am sandwiched in the middle. With walls at both the top and bottom of the bed, there was really only one option—up and over.

I decided to try to somehow throw my left leg over Mama without touching her and then balance long enough to get the rest of my body over hers and into freedom. I tried for almost *three hours*, but she was so large that it was impossible to get my leg over her without touching her. I contemplated doing so, but I just kept thinking, *If Dad wakes up and sees me straddling his wife, it's not going to be good.*

That was my first trip to Africa, and I had been right; it turned out to be totally uncomfortable. But that night, lying in the bed between a married couple I had just met, I started to understand that God often allows us to move into uncomfortable situations because he uses them to shape us more into the person he has created us to be. I would have never chosen to sleep in the middle of that couple, but I've noticed that just because a situation is uncomfortable doesn't necessarily mean it's wrong. I later learned that it is a great honor in that particular Zimbabwean village to share the family bed. I wish someone had told me at the time! It might have made things a bit less uncomfortable.

I've noticed that God has a habit of using our discomfort and impositions to position us for something more. I came home from that first trip to Africa and changed the course of my life. Within six months I had moved back to Zimbabwe to stay.

Now, I don't know about you, but I want to awake to God's use of uncomfortable situations to move me in the direction he wants me to go. The thing is, you just never know where you might wake up.

17

CLAIRE

A FEW MONTHS AGO, I attended a conference for Christian sports people. I usually prefer traveling to do stuff instead of just talking about doing stuff, but this was a unique event. Over seven hundred people from more than one hundred nations got together in Orlando for a week to discuss ideas on how to best leverage sports to reveal Jesus to others. I liked it. For at least four days.

The conference was held at the Florida Hotel and Conference Center. It's a good concept in theory; you can have a meeting in a conference room, at Starbucks, sitting by the pool, or while trying on a new suit at the Gap. The hotel is attached to the enormous Florida Mall.

But by day four, I had crossed the line. I had met my limit. I'd had my fill of meetings—and Cinnabon as well. I was ready to huddle with my own small group—just me, myself and I. So that morning I went down to breakfast just as I had done each day. I made small talk, ate some toast, and then, just before the start of the first session, I saw my opportunity—freedom was just outside the door. I scanned the room. I was confident no one would notice me. And that's when I did it; I made a break for the door.

As I ran through the large, ornately decorated lobby, I kept thinking to myself, *Why are you running? There's no need to run. No one is chasing you. And no one would care if they saw you leaving anyway.* Regardless, I still ran. I thought, *If someone does want to catch me, at least I should make it somewhat difficult by running as fast as I can.*

I arrived at the elevator out of breath but full of hope as I thought about a few hours spent alone, resting in my room. I caught my breath for a moment and then casually reached for the button marked "Up." Just as I did, *she* appeared.

She was dressed in a bright red blazer with a red skirt, red high heel shoes, and an equally bright red scarf meticulously tied around her neck. I figured she was auditioning for a role as Santa's helper in an upcoming Christmas play. But then I noticed the name tag attached to her lapel. It said, "Virgin Atlantic Airlines: CLAIRE."

Claire pulled a single carry-on-sized suitcase, and as we stood waiting for the elevator to pick us up, she was preoccupied with her phone. When the elevator arrived with a *bing*, Claire never looked up; she just walked on and continued looking at her phone.

So there we were, Claire and I, standing silently as the elevator began ascending toward our floor. All of a sudden, completely out of the blue, I surprised even myself when I looked directly at her, smiled, and said, "Hello, Claire!" Without missing a beat, Claire looked back at me, smiled, and said, "Hello, Aaron!" We both laughed, recognizing how helpful name tags can be when you meet.

———

Claire and I didn't speak long. Within a matter of seconds after our introduction, the elevator arrived at our floor. The doors opened, we looked at each other and politely smiled, and then we both quickly went our separate ways. I turned to the left and headed toward my room; Claire walked down the hall in the opposite direction, but then she looked back and said, "Oh, Aaron, I was going to ask, why are you in Orlando today?" I turned my head but continued to walk toward my room, responding, "Oh, I'm attending a conference for Christian sports people."

Out of the corner of my eye, I saw Claire let go of her suitcase and cover her mouth with her hands. So I stopped. Now slowly walking back in her direction, I asked, as respectfully as I could, "Claire, is something wrong?"

Her eyes were the size of space goggles and she was making an odd squealing noise as she dug her finger into her upper lip. I think she attempted some type of reply, but I can't say for sure. All I could make out were squealing sounds. So I just waited. She just kept squealing. So I just kept waiting.

I had been standing there for about a minute, when I asked again, "Claire, is everything all right?"

As Claire stared back at me, I had time to contemplate several scenarios as to what was going through her mind. When she finally removed her hands from her mouth and answered me, I was shocked by her reply. She looked around the hall, as if checking to ensure that no one was there, then leaned slightly toward me, like she was going to share her deepest secret, and whispered, "Are you a *Christian*?"

I wasn't sure how to respond. I've sat with Taliban leaders in Afghanistan and Muslim extremists in Sudan, Indonesia, and a host of other places you might not want to publicly call yourself a Christian. But this was Florida. I paused, and then said in a subdued voice, "Yes, that's right. I'm a Christian, Claire."

For the next thirty minutes Claire and I stood in the hall, telling each other our simple stories of faith. She had been an atheist for most of her forty years. She said, "I always thought Jesus was a psychological crutch for the weak. I wondered how people could believe in something they couldn't touch or see."

Claire had been firm in her belief, or rather unbelief, until six months prior to that moment in the hall, when a series of events caused her to start questioning her purpose and to wonder if there might be something more. She said, "I didn't tell my boyfriend or anyone in my family; I could barely believe it myself the first day I walked through the doors of that little church down the street from my house." It wasn't a Sunday when she visited. It was a Wednesday. A friend who knew her well had invited her to something called "Alpha" and described it as "An opportunity to explore the meaning of life."

Claire said she felt out of place at first. She didn't want to believe Jesus could possibly be real. "One day I was sitting in the back of the room, only moderately paying attention to the speaker, when suddenly I felt compelled to believe for the first time that Jesus is who he claimed to be—God," she said.

For several months following that moment at the church, the moment Claire described as a revelation, she tried her best to believe that Jesus was real, but everyone in her life kept saying, "Jesus is a myth, a farce, a fairy tale—he's not God, he was a man just like you and me."

So, on that very morning, she had decided that this was the day Jesus was either going to reveal himself to her or she would stop believing in him. She couldn't withstand the opposition any longer. So, on her way to work, she had prayed a desperate prayer. Claire said, "I was scared, but I had to know, so I prayed, 'Jesus, if you are real and worth trusting with my life, you are going to have to reveal yourself to me *today*!'"

She'd prayed that prayer as she drove to the airport in her hometown, Birmingham, England. She parked her car, moved through security, and then performed the duties of her job as a flight attendant during the eight hours it took to cross the Atlantic Ocean, from Birmingham to Orlando, Florida. As we spoke, Claire said, "I had totally forgotten I prayed that prayer today!" It was still morning in Orlando when her flight landed, but by the time the crew cleared customs, took the shuttle, and arrived at the hotel, it was already late at night in the UK.

That's when we met.

Claire and I only spoke for about thirty minutes that day. But the thing about our conversation that I will never forget, the image that is forever etched in my mind, is Claire, who kept saying with tears in her eyes, "I knew it. Jesus is real. Jesus is amazing!"

She kept saying it over and over.

"I knew it!"

"I *knew* it!"

"Jesus is real!"

"He's real!"

"Jesus is amazing!"

It wasn't the confession of someone who had made a cognitive decision or someone who was just going through the motions or casually following an unknown god but rather the desperate, emphatic, impassioned cry of someone who had genuinely seen and experienced Jesus.

I prayed a short prayer over Claire, gave her a hug, and walked to my room.

Now, I don't know about you, but I want to awake to God's desire to reveal himself and the outrageous things he is prepared to do to make that happen.

18

JESÚS CALLING

ROB LIVES WITH PYGMIES. Pygmies are a short, socially outcast group of jungle-dwelling, hunter-gatherer people. Rob is from Northern Ireland; the pygmies he lives with are from the Republic of Congo. He usually wears clothes; most of them do not.

A few months ago, I received a text message from Rob. It said,

Pygmies love soccer!

I had never been to the Republic of Congo, or hung out with any pygmies before, so I was intrigued.

I texted back.

And?

Apparently Rob had a plan.

> You should bring a team and come to the
> Republic of Congo to play soccer against the
> pygmies.

At the time, the Ebola virus was a hot topic and a localized civil war was happening a few hundred miles from the village where Rob lived. It didn't seem like a great idea to me. But Rob persisted.

> I just spoke with the village chief. He said if you
> visit, you can sleep in the village. It's a really
> great opportunity!

For the next several days Rob and I texted back and forth about the opportunity. The more I thought about it, the more I felt compelled to support Rob's work. He had only been living with the pygmies for a few months, and he was trying to build relationships with them. It didn't seem like the best timing, but Rob had left everything behind and moved his family from Northern Ireland to live among and share Jesus with the pygmies. A ten-day trip to the Republic of Congo to support their efforts seemed like the least I could do.

Now, playing soccer in the nude against a team of pygmies located eight hours into the Congolese jungle might not be for everyone, but I managed to find fifteen guys who thought it sounded like good fun. Perhaps the pygmies wouldn't make us play in the nude, but I figured everyone should be prepared, given the fact that Rob had said there was a real chance they would.

The night before our flight, the entire group was ready to go. Everyone had purchased their flights, received their immunizations, and collected the needed anti-malaria meds. We were packed and ready to go. One player had decided that since the pygmies play in the nude, he didn't need to pack many clothes, so he filled his suitcase with five hundred individually packaged Slim Jims instead.

The only problem was, I still didn't have my visa.

In order to obtain the necessary visa required to travel to the Republic of Congo, we had sent our passports to the Republic of Congo Embassy in Washington, DC. Even though I had sent my passport well in advance of everyone else, I was the only person in our group who had not received my passport back. I had no idea why, or where it might be.

Have you ever attempted to speak with someone at a government agency before? It's not easy. But, after a persistent effort, I managed to reach an actual person at the Congolese Embassy.

"Hello, this is Aaron Tredway. I'm supposed to go to Congo tomorrow but I haven't received my passport back from you. Can you tell me where it is?"

"Aaaahhhh . . . ummmm . . . mmmm . . ." said the lady on the other end of the phone. "Ah, ok, let me call you back," she said.

I'd just spent several hours trying to reach someone at the embassy, so I quickly said, "Nope, I need you to help me out. I can wait! I depart tomorrow. Just find out where it is. *Please.*"

She seemed to respond to my plea. "Ok, I'll help. Hold, please."

I waited on hold at least forty-five minutes, listening to recorded Congolese drum music, but I refused to hang up. Finally, the woman returned to the phone and said, "I found out the answer. We returned your passport two weeks ago. You must have it."

I tried my very best not to sound combative when I said, "Well, that's strange, because *I do not have it!*"

Apparently my passport had been lost, stolen, or otherwise misplaced.

With less than twenty-four hours until the flight, I didn't have many options. Conventional wisdom would suggest I wasn't going to Congo. But you never know what might happen when Jesus is involved.

I hung up the phone and sent a text message to our group.

> Well guys, it doesn't look like I'm going to Congo with you unless Jesus provides a way.

Given the circumstance, there was nothing to suggest that he would, but I figured I should at least ask.

I decided that if God wanted me to go to Congo, he would figure out a way and I would go. So that night I packed my suitcase, believing God could provide a way. I wanted to give Jesus every opportunity to provide, so I also decided to go to Washington, DC, the following morning and attempt to get a new passport, visa, and yellow fever card, all in the same day. On paper, it's impossible, but I just kept thinking, *You never know what might happen when Jesus is involved.*

That night before we went to sleep, Ginny and I prayed, "Jesus, do what only you can do if you want me to go to Congo with the team!" At four in the morning, I departed for my flight from Cleveland, Ohio, to Washington, DC.

I landed in Washington, DC, and by eight in the morning, I was in a taxi heading toward the US Bureau of Consular Affairs. On the way I tried to call the Department of State to plead my case, but no one answered the phone. Everything was automated. After several unsuccessful calls to multiple government agencies, I finally connected with a pleasant woman who seemed to have little authority. I shared my sob story about the Congolese Embassy losing my passport and my need to be in Congo with the rest of the team. It was all very moving. I think the woman might have even shed a tear on my behalf, but it didn't seem to help much as she then told me that the next available passport appointment was over three weeks away. Before I hung up, I said, "I know this is a crazy request, but if you can, please connect me with someone who would be able to help." She didn't promise much, but she did say, "I might know a guy. Let me see what I can do."

I arrived at the US Bureau of Consular Affairs on Pennsylvania Ave. and quickly joined the long line of people waiting to pass through the security checkpoint at the front of the building. I waited my turn, and when I arrived at the front of the line, I approached a large man in a blue suit. He had a silver badge on his chest and a gun holstered at his waist. "Hello, sir!" I said enthusiastically. "How are you today?"

"Appointment time?" he said with absolutely no facial expression.

"Yes, well, I'm here to get a new passport today, and I'm hoping you can help me!"

"Appointment time?" he said again. Still no facial expression.

"Ok, so, technically . . ."

"Next!"

Apparently there is no talking your way into a United States government building—*I tried*.

Despite my best efforts, I couldn't get in to plead my case. I didn't have an appointment. There didn't seem to be a way to obtain an appointment. And there didn't seem to be any exceptions.

I stood outside the US Bureau of Consular Affairs, watching hopeful applicants scurry into the warmth of the building and wondering what I should do. It was cold. I didn't know how long I could last outside. It wasn't snowing, but winter was definitely on its way. I decided to sit down on the pavement and wait as long as my extremities remained functional. Maybe God was intervening on my behalf and I just needed to wait a bit longer for him to show up.

After about an hour of sitting on the frozen gravel, I heard my phone ring. I didn't recognize the number but took the call anyway. A soft-spoken man with a prominent Spanish accent greeted me and said he had been contacted about a missing passport. I don't think the man ever mentioned his role with the government or what his official title was, but I wasn't too concerned. I was singularly focused and he seemed to be my only hope, however improbable that hope might have been.

As I explained my situation, he seemed empathetic. He wasn't emotional, or particularly interested in the details of the problem, but a few times he said, calmly, "I will help you." After a few minutes, he eventually said, "Ok, here's what you do. Go back into the Consular Affairs building and tell the man at the counter that I have authorized you to get a new passport today."

I was grateful for the phone call, and I didn't want to seem unappreciative, but I responded, "Sir . . . *that's never going to work!* You want me to casually walk up to a US government official and tell him that *you* authorize *me* to get a new passport, and just like that, they are going to do it?"

"Yes, that's right."

"What about the guards?"

"Tell the guards the same thing."

As much as I pressed for an alternate option, the man seemed entirely confident in his plan. He didn't go out of his way to assure me, he just said, "Trust me." I thanked him, and as we hung up the phone, I said, "Ok, I'm trusting you, but who should I say you are?"

"Just tell them Jesús sent you."

I probably should have been more excited when he mentioned his name, but he pronounced it the Spanish way, "HEH-soos," so I didn't really make the connection. I hung up the phone and walked back into the building. I'm sure the security guards must have been thinking, *You fool . . . we already sent you packing once today!* I waited in the line, and when I got to the front, I sheepishly told the guard, "I was told I could get a new passport today." No joke, the guard started laughing out loud and slapping his knee. He called to the other guard and said, "Hey, Jim, this guy thinks we are going to let him in just because he says so!" I didn't want to exacerbate the situation, but I interjected, "No, I didn't say so, but a man named Jesús called me and said he approves." I had literally no expectation that this would work, but upon hearing Jesús's name, the guards allowed me to pass without hesitation.

I was a bit confused by that interaction with the guards, but I didn't have time to ponder the situation as I walked into the building. Inside, people sat quietly, whispering things to the person next to them or playing with their phones. There wasn't much of a line, so I walked straight up to the counter and greeted the man behind the desk. "Hello, I was told I could get a new passport today," I said.

The man looked at me and pleasantly responded, "Not a problem. What time is your appointment?"

"Well, I don't have an appointment, but Jesús called me and said . . ."

I promise you, before I could get any further, the man behind the counter said, "*Jesús* called you?"

"Yes, he called me on the phone fifteen minutes ago and said I could get a new passport today." The man smiled widely. Looked across the desk. Motioned for me to listen closely. And then he said, "Young man, if Jesús is for you, then so am I."

And with that he told me to come back in two hours to collect my new passport.

Within twenty-four hours I received a new passport, a Congolese visa, a yellow fever card, and rebooked my flight for the following day from Washington, DC, to the Republic of Congo. That day in Washington, I was reminded again that when you are awake to Jesus's involvement, you never know what will happen. You might even learn some Spanish.

19

MAFIA PARTY

DANA IS ABOUT ONE THING—LOVE. Several years ago he created a registered organization called FLO—Forever Loving Others. As the only employee in the history of FLO, he was the CEO, CFO, COO, and the janitor all at the same time. One thing's for sure, the organization's vision was clear—*love others*. That was it.

I met Dana almost twenty years ago. He is one of my best friends. He's also one of my most unique friends. Those who know him would definitely agree; it's almost impossible to predict what Dana will do.

———

Several years ago one of the deadliest natural disasters in history, a tsunami, impacted fourteen nations in the southeast region of Asia. With over one hundred and seventy thousand lives lost,

Indonesia was one of the nations hardest hit. One day shortly after the disaster, Dana and I were talking about the tsunami when he said, "Dude, we need to go share some love with the people!" I assumed the more immediate need was to help with things like food, clothing, and shelter, but love is always good.

Dana persisted, "We just need to connect with people and love them, bro!"

I decided to explore some possibilities, and a few months later an Indonesian church invited me to bring our team to play soccer with the children of displaced families.

So we went to Indonesia. I brought some soccer balls, orange cones, and clothing we had collected to give away to the kids. Dana brought his guitar, a four-foot-tall gold cup trophy, an inflatable donkey, and a pink tuxedo. When I saw him walk into the airport the morning of our flight, he just looked at me, winked, and said, "Trust me, bro. I know what I'm doing."

The church served as an excellent host, and they assigned Mr. Amen to be our guide. To this day I'm still not sure if that was his real name, but it provided for some good conversation. One day Mr. Amen came into the large room the team was staying in at the church and said, "I have good news: you guys have been invited to play a soccer match against the best team in our region!" Mr. Amen seemed excited. "It will take us eight hours to drive there in the church van, but if we depart early tomorrow, we can make it."

Although we hadn't planned to make that trip, I thought, *We've been doing soccer clinics with kids every day for over a week. It could be good to change things up.* But before we committed, Mr. Amen noted, "Just be aware, the area where the team is located is strongly Islamic. The area we are visiting tomorrow is known to be very aggressive, so just don't mention Jesus's name and everything should be fine."

We all agreed. At least that's what I thought.

The next morning we woke up before sunrise and packed all of our gear, soccer balls, the four-foot gold cup trophy, and eighteen American-sized athletes into a twelve-passenger Asian-sized church van. In theory the van had air-conditioning, but I don't think that theory had been tested. We traveled eight hours along dirt and gravel paths, through dense vegetation and the damp humidity characteristic of that region. Hot, tired, and saturated by our own sweat, we arrived at the match just before the scheduled kickoff. I'm not sure what we expected, but it wasn't the fifteen thousand Indonesians who were anxiously waiting in the makeshift soccer stadium constructed entirely from bamboo and chicken wire.

Our opponent wasn't great. We won the game easily. But from time to time, throughout the match, I would look up from the field and think, *Wow, this is outrageous. We are playing in front of fifteen thousand Muslims in a remote part of the largest Muslim nation in the world.* We had gone to Indonesia to share our faith in Jesus, and even though we couldn't speak about him directly, we were building relationships with people. I kept thinking, *You never know what God will do.*

As the game concluded, Mr. Amen said, "I think you should share something encouraging with the people. So many of them lost a great deal in the tsunami." So one of our players stood on a small table in front of the main seating area and spoke, through a translator, to the people. We had all been told the crowd would be Muslim. We had all heard Mr. Amen say, "Don't talk about Jesus openly." I thought we all knew what to say in that situation.

I think we all did—everyone, that is, *but* the guy who stood on the table and spoke.

Standing in front of the large crowd, he said, "We have traveled a long distance to be here with you today. We want you to know that we are here because *Jesus* loves you!" When he said *Jesus*, the crowd began to cheer.

"We want you to know that Jesus loves you and he has a purpose for your life!" Again, a ripple of commotion pulsated through the crowd.

The guy from our team was breaking protocol but no one in the crowd seemed to mind—at least, that's what I thought in the moment. But what I failed to realize was that when the people heard Jesus's name, they weren't cheering for him, they were cheering *against* him—all *fifteen thousand* of them.

Somewhere between all the cheering, shouting, and the frenzy of the moment, an older man stepped out from the crowd of people and approached our coach. He spoke in a calm yet resolute manner and said, "If you mention Jesus's name again, we will make a bomb and blow you up."

And then he walked away.

By that point, most of the players had dispersed around the stadium. Some were signing autographs. Some were posing for photos. Several were letting pretty girls kiss them on their cheek. Our coach immediately started yelling, "Get on the bus! Everyone needs to get on the bus, *now!*"

It took several minutes, but we all got in the van and managed to leave the stadium before anything more serious occurred. Mr. Amen had been in the van talking on his phone during the commotion, so he was confused as to why we were speeding away. He said, "Guys, good news, we are going to dinner with the owner of the team!" There was really no time to protest. Within moments, we arrived at one of the largest houses I've ever seen.

We piled out of the van, marveling at the house and its surroundings as we walked toward the door. The house was like a setting from a fantasy movie. There were several guys standing by the gate, wearing black Kevlar jumpsuits and holding semi-automatic weapons. The sun had just set, but all of them were still wearing black sunglasses. As we walked in, Dana put me in a choke hold and said, "Bro, this is awesome. This guy has tigers and hyenas at his house!" We were shown to a large outdoor patio area and told to wait.

It was at this time that Mr. Amen decided to share a few more details about our host, the owner of the team we had just played. He looked around cautiously, and then, speaking in a low voice, he said, "Ok, guys, it's probably good to know that our host is a strong Muslim and also the head of the Indonesian mafia." I waited for him to smile and say, "Nah, just kidding!" He never did.

I wanted to get up and sprint as fast as possible toward our van, but I thought that might be too obvious. I sat there thinking, *What do we do? We just spoke about Jesus in front of fifteen thousand Muslims who chased us out of town, and now we're hanging out with the head of the Indonesian mafia.*

I leaned over to Dana, who was sitting to my right, and said, "Hey, we need to get out of here!" He just looked at me quizzically, and then he said, "Bro, why would we leave now? The party is just about to begin!"

"We need to go because this guy will know about what just happened at the stadium; he's a Muslim extremist, *and* it sounds like he's just an all-around bad dude!"

Dana wasn't buying it. He shook his head and said, "Bro, this is why we came. We've just got to *love* this guy!"

Now, I'm all for loving people, but in that moment I realized that it's much easier to love people who are likely to love you back.

Dana grabbed the back of my neck, uncomfortably pulled my forehead in so that it was touching his, and said, "Trust me. We got this. It's all about the love!"

After about an hour, the mafia boss finally appeared. I had never met a mafia boss, but he wasn't what I expected. He wore a white polo shirt, pink jeans, and white Sperry Top-Sider boat shoes. If he happened to be holding fifteen-pound dumbbells in each hand, he might have weighed one hundred pounds, which would mean he was quite large considering his four-foot-ten frame.

The man went around the room politely shaking everyone's hand, but to my horror, when he came to Dana he received Dana's infamous "glory shake" instead. You really need to see the glory shake to fully understand it, but it's essentially a greeting Dana has cultivated over the years. As Dana and the mafia boss were standing there face-to-face, Dana pointed to the sky and somehow convinced the mafia boss to do the same. As they were both pointing at the sky, Dana yelled, "Glory!" and then thrust his right arm in between the mafia boss's legs, grabbed hold of his backside belt loop, and then picked him up and held him upside down.

I've witnessed Dana glory-shaking the vice president of Nepal, the general of the Tajikistan army, a member of the Syrian Taliban, and an eighty-five-year-old Congolese pygmy chief. Most people don't know if they should laugh, cry, or kick Dana in the groin when he finally puts them down.

When Dana finally returned the mafia boss to solid ground, he just stood there staring at Dana. None of his crew said a word.

Dana didn't say anything either. He has a way of breaking you down like that. If nothing else, he just outwaits you. And then finally, after what seemed like forever, the mafia boss cracked a smile. Dana just kept waiting. The mafia boss smiled a bit more, and then all of a sudden he burst into laughter, and of course everyone else laughed too.

That night Dana wore his pink tuxedo and he kept calling the mafia boss "my twin" because of his pink pants. At various points he had the guards in their Kevlar suits bouncing around on his inflatable donkey, and toward the end of the night he awarded the mafia boss the four-foot-tall gold cup trophy for being "The best mafia boss in Indonesia."

What amazed me about that night was that, aside from the few tense moments immediately following the glory shake, our group of eighteen Jesus-loving soccer players from the United States had an amazing, positive time interacting with a group of Muslim extremists from the Indonesian mafia. The contrast from the stadium to the house was night-and-day different. At the stadium we chose to speak about the love of Jesus and we were chased out of town, but at the mafia boss's house we demonstrated the love of Jesus and were embraced with open arms.

Around three in the morning, I did end up sharing my story of faith in Jesus with the mafia boss, and he shared about his beliefs as well. He didn't make a radical conversion or turn from his life of crime on the spot, but I believe God uses those seeds of faith planted and watered by love.

Now, many years later, we are still in communication with that mafia boss. He's not yet connected his life to Jesus, but he has turned from his life of crime. Perhaps he has learned something from us over the years. I know God used that night, and Dana, to teach me that *love* is one of the most powerful tools around.

I've noticed you never know what might happen when you respond to others in love. That night at the mafia boss's house we ate, drank, laughed, sang, and danced together. We even rode on the elephants that lived in his personal zoo.

I don't know about you, but I want to awake to the power of love. When that happens, there's no telling what God will do.

20

PUBLIC SHOWER

WHEN I WAS A KID I had a life-size picture of Magic Johnson hanging in my room. Magic was my favorite basketball player on my favorite team, the Los Angeles Lakers, but more importantly he epitomized most of what I wanted to be. Of course, I didn't know Magic; I only knew what I read or saw on TV, but he seemed like a cool guy. He drove a nice car, lived the celebrity life, and got paid to play basketball and live in LA. That seemed good enough to me.

I never formally wrote down my definition of success; the picture of Magic Johnson on my wall was all the definition I needed.

A few years ago I was in Bangkok, Thailand, to play in a goodwill soccer match against the Thailand National Soccer Team.

The match was supposed to be held at the newly built National Sports Stadium and broadcast live on TV.

On the day of the match, our team got on the bus, drove through Bangkok traffic, and arrived at the stadium several hours before the start. I didn't have many expectations, other than I knew it was supposed to be a "friendly match," but when we arrived at the stadium, I remember thinking, *This stadium looks like trash.*

I didn't want to seem ungrateful, so I wasn't going to share my thoughts out loud, but that's about the time when one of my teammates said, "Hey, did you hear this is the oldest stadium in town?" Apparently the new stadium was not yet complete, so our game had been relocated to a facility built during the Cold War. Rumor had it that this stadium was scheduled to be demolished the next week.

Regardless of the state of the venue, hundreds of Thai people were waiting to greet us at the gate. And despite pouring rain, thousands more filled the stadium prior to the start of the match. For a friendly game, our hosts seemed quite official. A Thai boy-band sang the national anthem. There was a coin toss at center field, and even a mock kickoff by some political person wearing a black-and-white tuxedo.

At halftime our team was losing by three goals. The second half only got worse. By the end of the game we had not only lost but were also soaking wet, embarrassed, and covered in red dirt.

I was the first one into the locker room because I didn't have much time before my flight back to the United States later that night. I needed to take a shower, change my clothes, and head for the airport as fast as I could.

The locker room was cold, drab, and damp. It was similar to what I'd imagine a medieval torture chamber to be like. I didn't see a guillotine, but then again, I didn't have time to look.

I got undressed, threw my muddy uniform in a plastic bag, and headed into the enormous open shower room. Standing under a rusted showerhead, I turned the knob but nothing happened. By that point all the guys had started filtering into the locker room, and they probably heard me yell, "Come on!" as I tried several different showers. I was getting colder by the second. I tried every shower in the room. Every single one was the same—rusted and without water. *Now what?* I thought. *There's no way I can fly over twenty-four hours back to the United States like this.* There had to be a solution; I just didn't know what it was.

Someone found a janitor. I didn't have much time left when I approached him and said, "Shower?" Of course, he only spoke Thai, so he stared at me blankly. I said again, "Sir, I need a shower." He still didn't understand. Finally, I pulled him into the shower room and showed him the problem. That's when his face lit up.

It seemed he wanted me to follow him, so I tightened the towel around my waist and we began winding our way through the stadium halls. Eventually we found a public restroom and the janitor pointed toward a hose. It wasn't in a shower stall, or a locker room, or even a sink; it was attached to a wall in the middle of the restroom.

I shook my head—*no.* But the janitor smiled and shook his head—*yes.* I waved my hands and pointed outside the door, but the janitor seemed adamant and time was running out. I decided to go for it.

So there I was.

Standing naked in a public restroom.

With the janitor, a bar of soap, and a hose attached to a wall. That's when I thought, *I bet this never happened to Magic Johnson!*

As I turned on the hose, I was happy it worked. Unfortunately, at the same time, several unsuspecting men walked into the restroom as well. I'm not sure if the initial shock was more awkward for me or them, but it only got worse.

As I was attempting to quickly scrub the mud off my body, about six more guys came in. And then it happened. I'm not sure who it was. I don't know who said it. But someone pointed at me and said, "*Goalie!*" And that's when things got wacky.

Although I was completely wet and naked, it made no difference to these guys. There was no shame among those men. Several of them pulled out their cell phones and their digital cameras. A few started to come toward me, like they wanted me to pose with them in a photo. The selfie hadn't been discovered at that point, but there was definitely the same vibe.

Once the cameras came out, there was no time to waste. The only thing I could think to do was to put my thumb over the end of the hose, like I did when I was a kid, and scream as loud as I could while I squirted every guy within range. It worked! Within seconds all the paparazzi had left the building.

Mildly traumatized, I got back to the locker room, got dressed, and jumped into a taxi to head to the airport. After the horrible game and the incident in the restroom, I was ready to just sit in the taxi and decompress. But just as I sat down the taxi driver looked at me in his rearview mirror and said, "Hey, you goalie. I know you. *Goalie!*" Apparently he had seen the game on TV. He also spoke some English. It seemed like a bad combination for me.

I wasn't in the mood to chat, but the taxi driver persisted. "Goalie, bad game! *Very* bad game," he said. He wasn't making things any easier.

So, after trying to deflect the conversation for several minutes, I decided there was no option. I was a captive audience. And maybe so was he.

"So, what's your name?" I said.

"I'm Mr. Dao."

"Ok, Mr. Dao, tell me, have you ever had a bad day?"

"Oh, yes. Many bad days," he said.

"So, what do you do when you have a bad day? How do you deal with it?"

Mr. Dao didn't say anything for about a minute, and then he said, "I don't know. I guess I just hope karma will be better the next day."

From the backseat of his taxi, I made eye contact with Mr. Dao in his rearview mirror, and then I said, "Mr. Dao, like you said earlier, today has been a very bad day for me, but my *hope* for tomorrow is not in fate; it's in a person named Jesus. Because of my relationship with Jesus, I don't have to carry the burden of my bad day; Jesus will carry it for me."

I didn't expect to have a two-hour conversation about Jesus with my taxi driver on the way to the airport. But I did. And just before he dropped me off, Mr. Dao said, "Goalie, I would like to know your Jesus too!"

Growing up I had a picture of success that I hung on my bedroom wall. Success drove a nice car. Success lived a celebrity life. Success never failed. But I've noticed that my picture of success doesn't always match God's.

Jesus's first followers weren't the most educated, talented, or impressive bunch. They were often misunderstood, mistreated, and persecuted. The apostle Paul was beaten with rods, pelted with stones, shipwrecked, robbed, chased, starved, and imprisoned—but the thing is, God used Paul and each of the first followers of Jesus to radically change the world. I'd call that success.

A few weeks after I got home from Thailand, a teammate sent me a picture of me standing in that public restroom, holding the hose, with a towel around my waist (fortunately). For many years I had that picture hanging on my office wall. It's not Magic Johnson and it doesn't depict a perfect day, but was it a successful day? I'd say yes!

I don't know about you, but I want to awake to a new picture of success. But when you do, just remember: bring a loofah.

21

CYCLE FOR HOPE

ROB IS ONE OF THOSE PEOPLE who thinks outside the box. Sometimes I wonder how he developed his unique perspective. He might have been born that way. But I think it's more likely connected to his childhood, which was spent on an island off the coast of the poorest country in Africa, Guinea Bissau. His family was the first white family to arrive on the island, and because there were no other white people around, Rob spent much of his childhood believing he was black.

A few years ago he called and said, "Hey, we should go for a bike ride." Neither Rob nor I cycled much, but I thought it could be fun. "Where do you want to ride?" I said.

"I was thinking we could do Africa, maybe."

I should have known Rob wouldn't be suggesting a leisurely pedal through the park.

Rob didn't own a bicycle the day he called to suggest we ride through Africa. And to be clear, he didn't want to ride *across* Africa, he wanted to ride *down* it—ten thousand, four hundred, and eighty-seven miles from the top to the bottom of the continent.

"Why do you want to ride through Africa, Rob?"

"I don't know; it just seems like an outrageous thing to do!"

"Couldn't we just run with the bulls in Pamplona or try to climb a tall mountain somewhere?" I said.

"Well, we could, but I want to cycle for a purpose. I want to share Jesus with all the different people we meet along the way."

I liked the concept, but there were many unknowns. At the time, I couldn't even imagine everything we'd need to do in order to orchestrate such an outrageous event.

"Ok, let's say we were going to attempt to cycle across Africa, where would we even begin?"

"We should probably buy a bike!"

Rob was the visionary and champion of this outrageous event we called the Cycle for Hope. At various points throughout the two years it took to plan the trip, I called Rob with questions like, "What will we eat? Where will we sleep? Who will ride with us? What if a wild animal chases us? What if we get really sick? What if we are stranded somewhere with no cell phone reception?" Rob's response was always the same: "I guess we'll just figure it out."

One day, a few months before we were scheduled to meet in Tangier, Morocco, to begin the trip, I called Rob and said, "Do you have a strategy for how we are going to share Jesus with the people we meet?"

170

I'm a bit more type A than Rob; I needed some details.

"Not exactly."

"Well, what does that mean?"

"It just means life doesn't always require a full manuscript. Sometimes it's just best to just let things rise out of the unknown."

That's never my first thought. I wouldn't describe myself as rigid, but I like to have a clear plan, a strategy, or at least a picture of how I will accomplish the objectives of anything I do. But this trip was Rob's thing, not mine; I was just along for the ride.

"Ok," I said. "Let's see what the unknown brings our way!"

When it came time to commit, I couldn't be away for the entire seven months Rob thought it would take to complete the ride. But I committed to riding with the group of ten core riders for the first month. Africa is extremely diverse in more ways than one. At many points along the ride, the temperature would be over 120 degrees, but as we prepared the bikes that first morning, the temperature was just below freezing. I only had one thought: *I knew these spandex shorts weren't going to be enough!*

"Hey, guys, c'mon over," said Rob in his characteristic Irish accent.

We all huddled together on a small patch of frozen dirt. The sun was just rising, and Rob prayed, "Jesus, we don't know what you will do, but we pray, meet with us and others as we go."

That was it. Everyone said a hearty "Amen!" and we set off.

There was a lot of banter that first day. Everything was new. Everything was fresh. Everything seemed exciting. Several people had a bike odometer attached to their handlebars. After about five minutes, exactly one mile into the ride, one of the core cyclists yelled from the back in a jovial demeanor, "Hey, everyone, we only have ten thousand, four hundred, and *eighty-six* miles to go!" Everyone cheered wildly.

I rode in the back of the pack with Rob most of the first day. He liked to keep an eye on everyone as cars recklessly zipped past us, leaving very little margin for error. At one point an eighteen-wheel truck drove by us going at least ninety miles per hour on a winding seaside road. That was the first of many times I prayed, "Jesus, protect us as we ride!" It's amazing how much time you have to think and pray when you are sitting on a bike for ten to twelve hours each day.

As the sun began to set that evening, Rob called out, "What do you guys think about that field over there?" It seemed like a fine field to me. The thing is, I didn't realize that's where Rob wanted to *sleep*.

So that's where we stopped after twelve hours of cycling on day one—in a random cornfield, on the side of a road, in Africa.

The next several weeks were exactly the same. It was like *Groundhog Day*—we woke before the sun rose, consumed as much food as we could, rode for twelve hours, and then found a field without running water, toilets, showers, or any other amenity you might desire.

One day we were cycling through the middle of nowhere in Senegal. Rob and I were enjoying the desolation of our surroundings, with very few cars passing by. Our group was several miles in front of us because the two of us were busy philosophizing about what to do if we happened to be chased by a bear. There are no bears in Africa, but at least it helped us pass the time, even if it slowed us down.

As we cycled, a group of kids playing soccer caught our eye. And even though we were now some distance behind our group, Rob said, "What do you think? Should we stop and play?"

I'm sure the kids thought we were some type of extraterrestrial beings as we pulled up to their game wearing our bike shorts, helmets, and identical florescent cycling shirts. We even had antennas in the form of the tubes attached to the water pouches strapped to our backs.

We got off our bikes, and all the kids stopped playing and started to stare. Rob said in French, "Hello, kids, what do you think? Can we join your game?"

For a moment the kids didn't say a word, but then one of the bigger boys passed me the ball. I was wearing my cycling shoes, but I showed them a few tricks. Within minutes we were all playing together, right there, on the side of the road.

As we were running up and down the dirt field, Rob passed me the ball and said, "We can't play too long. Let's just stay until one of us scores a goal." It turns out that it's not as easy as you would think to score a goal when you are wearing bike shorts, a helmet, and cycling shoes—even if the competition is only twelve years old.

We never did score a goal, but the game came to an end. I was walking toward my bike when I heard Rob gather all the kids and then say, "I want to tell you a story."

It wasn't a long story, but the kids listened intently as Rob shared about his life. He said, "You can see that I'm a white guy, but I'm really African just like you!" All the kids laughed. For the next ten minutes, Rob shared about his childhood on the island, his love of soccer, and how he met Jesus when he was around their age, and how that meeting totally changed Rob's life. I don't speak French, so I only found out what Rob shared when he told me later, but I do know what I saw. At a certain point, when Rob asked, "Boys, do any of you want to invite Jesus into *your* life?" all twenty of the boys raised their hands.

I left the cycle shortly after that day, but the core team carried on. Along the way they had to evade land mines and were stopped by a large herd of elephants; they were also mugged, stranded, and attacked by an eighty-year-old man with a stick. As *planned*, the group never knew what any particular day might bring, but they offered *hope* wherever they went.

While I was with the group we visited orphanages, schools, churches, and several NGOs. The group also shared their faith on the radio and several times on TV. After ten thousand, four hundred, and eighty-seven miles, one hundred and ninety-five days, seventeen countries, and countless bucket showers, Rob and the group encountered one of the only predetermined points of the trip: the finish line, in Cape Town, South Africa. I was there the day they rode in.

A few months after the outrageous adventure had concluded, Rob and I were sitting on my back porch. I said, "Rob, what's the most important thing that you learned on the Cycle of Hope?"

Rob looked at me and said, "Aaron, I can't explain it, but I know for sure that God can, will, and does meet us in the unknown."

For a person like me, that's not always easy to accept. I like to plan, organize, and, when possible, script whatever I do. I like to feel safe, secure, and in control. But the thing is, I'm not God. I don't always know his thoughts or the ways he might want to work, the people he might want me to meet, or what he might want me to do.

When you awake to the unknown you might not be able to predict what will happen, but maybe that's the point.

22

VIRAL OPPOSITION

A FEW MONTHS AFTER Ginny and I walked down the aisle on our wedding day, I received an email from a brick maker and another man named Pastor Football. The pair asked if I would visit them in Kathmandu, Nepal. I had never met a brick maker or a pastor of football, so I decided it was a good thing to do.

Nepal is home to eight of the top ten highest mountains in the world: Everest, Kangchenjunga, and Annapurna, to name a few. It's also referred to as the world's only Hindu kingdom, statistically less than one percent Christian. Regardless, the brick maker and Pastor Football had a plan to share Jesus in their nation, and their email suggested they needed some help: "Dear Mr. Aaron, please kindly consider coming to the beautiful Himalayan nation, Nepal. We need you to help our Church." They spelled "church" with a capital "C," so I was assuming they didn't mean one church but rather many. "Our Church is small but vibrant; we want to share the hope we have found in Jesus with our nation. We have heard you know how to share Jesus through soccer."

The plan wasn't elaborate. Their request was simple: cast a vision to their church in Nepal for sharing Jesus through soccer, and show them how to do it. I thought, *This shouldn't be difficult. I have helped several churches around the world create a vision and strategy for sharing Jesus through soccer.*

The problem was, I didn't anticipate how the church in Nepal would respond.

I arrived in Kathmandu on a sweltering summer afternoon; it had to be at least one hundred and ten degrees. The brick maker met me at the airport, hugged me like we were long-lost brothers, and smeared some red clay substance over my forehead and on my nose. "Welcome, brother!" he exuberantly proclaimed as he wrapped a thick yellow scarf around my neck. "You are an official Nepali now!" he said as we jumped in his car.

We met Pastor Football at the brick maker's favorite restaurant in downtown Kathmandu. They called it a restaurant, but it seemed more like a cave to me—it was dark, damp, and underground, and the walls were jagged rock. In between large bites of lentil soup and rice, Pastor Football said, "So, tell us, how do we share Jesus through soccer?"

I said, "Well, that depends on who you are trying to reach."

That afternoon we sat in the cave eating our lentils and talking about Hindu culture in Nepal. We also spoke about how the government wanted to be officially recognized as a Hindu kingdom and how it wasn't illegal to share the gospel in Nepal but that Hindus didn't want to talk about Jesus, so the church had struggled to grow. Pastor Football said, "Our churches have tried many different things to share Jesus with our Hindu friends. We stand on the street and hand out information, but we usually find those papers in the trash. We've held some concerts with Christian bands, but only Christian people seem to come. We've even paid to have a radio show, but I'm not sure if anyone listens."

It was a short visit, but a plan was set in motion for how we could show the church in Nepal how to share Jesus through soccer.

I returned to Nepal four months later, accompanied by my friend Dana, a horn he called a *shofar*, and fifteen other soccer players from the organization I work with, Ambassadors Football. Upon our arrival we took a twelve-hour bus ride to the second largest city in the country, a place called Pokhara.

Pokhara is located at the base of Annapurna, in the Himalayas. It is a popular tourist destination because of the Himalayan trekking tours that begin from that city. As our bus pulled into town, we noticed a large sign hanging from a tree on one of the biggest streets. It said, "Welcome Christian Soccer Friends," and it had pictures of our faces scattered around the words. The church in Pokhara was obviously excited that we were there, but I decided I needed to have a chat with its leaders about strategy—when and how to share our faith with others. The night was full, but I should have remembered to do that.

As the sun was setting, *every* Christian in the town—roughly one hundred of the three hundred thousand people—gathered in a small building outside of town. We sang songs of worship. We ate. And we talked about some of the ways we've seen God use soccer to provide opportunity to share Jesus with others.

It was a good night. The church was enthusiastic. We all agreed to meet at the soccer stadium the next day.

The Pokhara soccer stadium is literally at the base of Anna-purna, and as we drove through the gate I saw the sun reflecting off the snowcapped peak that would provide the backdrop for our game. I thought to myself, *Majestic*. Sometimes there's nothing else you can say.

As spectators started to arrive at the stadium, I noticed several people whom we had met at the church the night before. Some were sitting, but I was surprised to see many of them walking around the stands, attaching enormous banners to the walls. By the time the match began, there must have been twenty different banners interspersed around the stadium, depicting different messages of faith for anyone in attendance to see.

The first banner that caught my attention had a life-size photo of *me*. On the side of my giant head, a caption said, "Jesus loves you, this I know, for the Bible tells us so!"

Another banner had a photo of Dana, with this caption: "Jesus: the way and the truth and the life!"

Every banner hanging around the stadium had a picture of one of our team members and an expression about Jesus's love, character, or purpose. We hadn't discussed that strategy the night before, but the congregation obviously had a plan of their own. I didn't think it was the best plan, but it seemed harmless enough. In the moment, I didn't consider the twenty-five million Hindu people who might not feel the same.

———

The game was fairly calm; people came, watched, and went. But just after we got back to our hotel, I received a call from the brick maker.

"Hello, Brother Aaron?"

"Yes, hello, brick maker, we won the game!"

"Hello, Brother Aaron."

"Yes, I can hear you, brick maker, how are you?"

"Um, yes, Brother Aaron . . . *we* have a problem."

"A problem?"

"Yes, I think Nepal is very angry with you."

I figured I had misunderstood when he'd said, "*Nepal* is very angry," so I said, "Did you mean there is a person who's upset?"

"No . . . [long pause] I mean the entire *nation!*"

I decided I better return to Kathmandu immediately.

I took a six-passenger plane back to the capital. The brick maker and Pastor Football met me at the airport. This time there was no red clay on the face, yellow scarf, or hugging, but there were plenty of questions.

"What happened at the game?"

I wasn't sure what they were referring to. People came to watch. We played. We won. We went back to the hotel. It seemed fairly routine to me.

"Why did you hang those signs around the stadium?"

"Signs?"

"Yes, there was a reporter from the largest Hindu magazine in Kathmandu. He was at the game. He took photos of your signs, the ones with your players' faces and the messages about Jesus. He wrote an article and posted it online during the game. The title of the article is, 'Exactly Who Is Ambassadors FC?'"

"Well, those weren't our signs. The church people made those signs and hung them in the stadium. We didn't have anything to do with it."

Apparently it didn't matter who was to blame. Nepal is one of the highest per capita social media users. The article had already gone viral.

I sat in a conference room, thinking about what to do. We could call a press conference and explain the banners weren't ours. Or maybe we could call the reporter who wrote the article and tell him our side of the story. But before I could formalize a plan, the brick maker received a call from the president of the soccer federation. "Tell Aaron I want to see him immediately!" he said.

We arrived at the soccer federation office thirty minutes later, and when we entered the president's office, he wasn't happy.

"I took a risk bringing you to Nepal to play against our teams, and you tricked me!"

"Sir, respectfully, we didn't attempt to trick you. Those weren't our banners."

At that point, I don't think he cared whose banners they were.

"Do you know my brother is the head of the Hindu party, campaigning to become the president of Nepal? This looks very bad that I brought you Christians here and you took advantage of our hospitality!"

The gravity of the situation was starting to sink in. It's not illegal to share the gospel in Nepal, but the soccer president felt he had been shamed. His veins were bulging from his neck as he continued to yell at me. I sat there contemplating different scenarios. *We are definitely going to prison*, I thought. *Ok, well, maybe not everyone will go to prison if we are lucky—maybe just me. Or, maybe, since it's not illegal to share the gospel in Nepal, we'll just be deported. I'd settle for deportation.*

As much as I tried to explain the banners weren't ours, it didn't matter. The president kept saying, "Someone must be held responsible." By default, I guess that person was me.

Four months prior, the brick maker, Pastor Football, and I had created a plan to help make Jesus known, and ultimately, to help the church in Nepal to grow.

I felt like we had failed.

I felt like I had failed.

I was embarrassed.

I was ashamed.

I wanted to apologize to whomever I needed to and then leave Nepal. But the thing is, you just can't predict what God will use, how he will work, or when he'll take your imperfect effort and transform it into something more.

After three hours with the president of the soccer federation, we came to an agreement. No one had to go to jail and our team would be permitted to stay according to our plan, but we weren't allowed to talk about Jesus in public or play any more matches in front of spectators, who would likely be participating in the numerous tweets, blogs, and discussion boards about our team, Ambassadors FC.

The final night of our time in Nepal, we had dinner with thirty pastors from Kathmandu. Although we had enjoyed our time, it didn't feel like we had accomplished any of our goals. So as we were finishing our food, I stood up at the head of the table and said to my new friends, "Brothers, on behalf of Ambassadors FC, I want to apologize that we couldn't help you to make Jesus known."

I had planned to say more, but immediately the head of the association of churches stood and said, "Aaron, please sit down." He then stood up and walked to the head of the table, paused, and said, "We pastors have been discussing your trip to Nepal and though you feel like you didn't accomplish your goal, *we* believe your trip has been even more than we had hoped."

As I was sitting there I thought, *How could that be? We totally failed. We played one game and then we were banned from sharing our faith in Jesus with others. We wanted to cast vision. We wanted to demonstrate to the church the power of soccer. We wanted to see God move in an outrageous way—but he didn't!*

It was as if the pastor at the front of the table heard my thoughts, because then he said, "I know you feel like you have failed us, and maybe you feel like you have failed God, but you should know that because of your visit, for the first time in the history of Nepal, millions of Hindu people in our country are discussing Jesus as they have never done before."

That was the beginning of Ambassadors Football Nepal. Today Ambassadors Football is an officially registered NGO in Nepal. The church is still small, but growing, and they are now using soccer as one of their primary tools to make Jesus known.

I want to awake to unexpected outcomes, because you never know when twenty-six million people might be watching.

23

THE RIOT

STEPHEN AND JOSH are two ordinary guys. They both grew up in the United States. They both played soccer in college. They both graduated. They both wanted to use their passion and talent to serve God and others in some tangible way. And somehow, they both found their way to Kawangware, one of the largest slums in Africa.

Kawangware is located on the outskirts of Nairobi, Kenya, and while poverty is a challenge no matter where you live, in Kawangware it's an epidemic. Roughly eight hundred thousand people live on an average of less than one dollar per day in Kawangware, which seems to also foster additional challenges. Teen pregnancy, prostitution, rampant crime, gangs, drugs, and infectious diseases like HIV/AIDS are also an issue.

Stephen and Josh wanted to make a difference.

I met Stephen and Josh when they were both nineteen years old. They dreamed of becoming famous soccer players, but they also wanted to use their lives for the glory of God. When we met, I couldn't have predicted that they would leave their friends, family, and the comforts of home to start a soccer team in the heart of Kawangware, but I'm sure they couldn't have either. Even though both had signed professional soccer contracts in the United States, they both heard about the need in Kawangware and decided to bring the hope of Jesus into that community, and that soccer would be an effective vehicle for doing so.

So they left everything, compelled by the belief that God had called them—and neither with much more than a desire to serve God and the people of Kawangware.

A few days after Stephen and Josh arrived in Kawangware, they called me on the phone.

"Aaron, we made it! We are here in Kawangware," Stephen shouted into the phone. It seemed to be a poor connection. But then again, they weren't calling from a high rise on the Upper East Side of Manhattan; they were calling from a pay phone, on the side of a dirt road, in a slum. Regardless, I shouted back, hoping they could hear me.

"Great! So how are you going to get started?"

"I don't know," Stephen replied. "That's what we're hoping that you could tell us."

Apparently Stephen and Josh didn't have much of a plan. They wanted to address some of the rampant social injustices and serve people in their new community, but they had no clue where to start.

I didn't know exactly what to tell them, but I've noticed sometimes you just need to start doing *something*; the details work themselves out.

As we were hanging up the phone, I said, "Maybe start by joining a local soccer team. Build some friendships and see where that goes."

"Ok," Stephen said. "We'll try!"

A few weeks later I got the news that Stephen and Josh had joined the Kawangware professional soccer team. Now, I'm not sure if *professional* was the correct term, as the players had to buy their own uniforms, rarely got paid, and almost always took public transportation to their games, but that's what the locals called it, and they asked Stephen and Josh to join their team.

Stephen and Josh integrated into the fabric of the slum quickly, as very few outsiders have ever done. They didn't just play soccer; they shared life with their new friends. Most foreigners wouldn't enter certain areas of the slum because of the very real danger they might meet, but Stephen and Josh walked wherever they chose to go without ever being mugged, bullied, or harassed in any way. They often visited their teammates' families for meals in their homes, and at times they would even spend the night, sharing a space on the floor of a tin-walled shack.

After only one year in Kawangware, Stephen and Josh learned that their soccer team didn't have enough financial resources to continue as it was. So they called me and said, "Hey, Aaron, what do you think about us purchasing the team and running it ourselves?"

Aside from the fact that Stephen and Josh had gone to Africa when they were twenty-two and had no money or experience and little knowledge about what it would take to own and operate a professional soccer team, I still thought it might be a good idea. I knew it wouldn't be easy, but I responded, "Guys, as long as you realize this could be extremely difficult, I think we should try!"

I flew in to meet with the man who owned the team. As we had a coffee in his office, he said, "Aaron, make me an offer. I'm ready to get rid of the financial burden of owning this team." So, after some discussion and a bit of negotiation on my part, we came to an agreement. We shook hands. And then we signed some papers to become the owners of a Kenyan soccer team—for exactly one dollar. Stephen became the general manager of the team and central midfield player. Josh was the director of community development and the center of defense.

It took the pair one year to raise the operational budget, rebrand, reimagine, and relaunch the team now called the Nairobi City Stars. And after all their commitment, hard work, and dedication, the first game of the new season in their new stadium, located in the heart of Kawangware, finally arrived. It seemed the guys had thought of everything; it was all in order. Although they couldn't have known what the opposing fans would do.

I was honored to attend the Nairobi City Stars' first game, held in Kawangware. The stadium was constructed entirely of chicken wire and white plastic chairs, but people still came out in droves.

Just before the start of the game, I walked into the stadium and noticed people chanting, dancing, and drinking lots of beer. I walked past one particularly inebriated guy, who kept yelling at me, "Hello, Mr. White Man. Did you know that I can fly?" Stephen waved to me from the side of the field, so I made my way past several thousand fans whose faces looked like Play-Doh being forced through a pasta maker because they were pressed so hard against the chicken wire.

I found Stephen sitting in a section marked "VIP," and when I walked up he said, "Hey, man, I saved you a seat." I was impressed with the whole affair; even though the VIP sign was written in crayon on a single sheet of notebook paper and hung on a tree, I really didn't care.

At halftime everything seemed to be going fine. The score was tied 0–0, and the enthusiastic crowd seemed happy enough. But shortly into the second half, after the Nairobi City Stars scored a goal, the opposing fans became noticeably annoyed and their irritation started to show.

With fifteen minutes left in the game, and the Nairobi City Stars up one goal to zero, I was still thinking anyone could win. But then, all of a sudden, without any warning at all, the fans of the opposing team started to shout and scream, and then they started shaking the fence that separated the spectators from the field. I can't pinpoint the trigger, but within minutes of the start of all the shouting, screaming, and shaking of the fence, things escalated into a full-blown riot.

In the blink of an eye the fans tore down the entire fence and thousands of people began flooding onto the field. White plastic chairs began to fly through the air. Men were throwing rocks and punching each other in the face. Women were running with small children attached to their backs, looking for a place to hide.

Amid the chaos, Stephen and I found Josh. Stephen yelled over all the noise, "What do you guys think we should do?"

Josh responded, "Maybe we should try to stop the people from destroying the rest of our field?"

I didn't want to be the bearer of bad news, but I thought, *If we try to stop this riot, it will literally be two thousand heavily intoxicated men against Stephen, Josh, and me.*

As we were debating options and I was thinking we didn't have much choice, someone threw a rock from somewhere near center field. It hit Josh in the back, causing him to immediately scream, "*Run!*"

So there we were, Stephen, Josh, and I, lying facedown in the dirt behind a little green bush on the side of the field. Stephen and I were wearing suits and dress shoes, but our least concern was a possible dry-cleaning bill. I'm not usually a nervous person and I wasn't overly concerned for myself, but as we huddled in the dirt behind that bush, I was praying, *God, I pray that no one dies.*

After about five minutes we came out from our cover. It seemed that just as fast as the riot had begun, it had concluded. When the police showed up, people scattered in every direction, leaving Stephen, Josh, and me standing in the middle of the obliterated soccer stadium with thousands of empty beer bottles—and nothing else.

When we went back to the house that night we didn't say much, but the next morning we all got up, made some strong coffee, and decided to chat.

Sitting there in the living room on a musty, plush green couch, I broke the silence when I said, "Guys, about yesterday. I really don't know what to say."

I thought that the discussion would be fairly straightforward. After all Stephen and Josh had done—their commitment, hard work, and dedication to the people of Kawangware—and after all they had left behind—their friends, family, and professional soccer careers—I thought to myself, *It would be perfectly legitimate if these guys said, "Forget these people, this team, and our desire to bring the hope of Jesus to this community. We don't need this. We can just go home."*

The tension in the room was palpable as we stared at the floor in silence. But after several minutes, Stephen finally said, "I can't speak for Josh, but yesterday was one of the worst days of my life. All of our work, everything we have done, all the effort we have poured into this project for an entire year was destroyed. I'm angry. I'm frustrated. I'm annoyed. But I still know that God is in control, and he can use this horrible event for his glory."

I was shocked that Stephen would say that. And just as shocked when Josh agreed.

Stephen and Josh refused to give up.

That day we prayed together, got up from the musty green couch, and agreed to rebuild.

I flew home a few days later, but Stephen and Josh stayed in Kawangware to continue what they had begun. As a result, countless people have encountered the hope of Jesus. Some have been set free from addiction to drugs or alcohol, and others have been spared from a life of crime or something worse. In the face of hardship, Stephen and Josh could have easily left their vision behind, but I've noticed that when people believe God is in control, unwavering resolve is often what you find.

Both Stephen and Josh met their wives in Kenya. And now, eight years later, Josh is serving God and others through coaching soccer in California, while Stephen and his wife continue to offer the hope of Jesus to the many people in Kawangware who are desperately in need. Stephen would tell you, "It's not always easy, but if God has called you to serve in a particular way, Jesus will provide the strength to keep going, even if your stadium happens to be torn down today."

Now, I don't know about you, but I want to awake to unwavering resolve. After all, if God is for us, who can be against us?

24

RUNNING STATUES

GROWING UP, I always thought my dad was normal.
I've since realized he is not. Every day, rain or shine,
for as long as I can remember, my dad has gotten
out of bed by four in the morning, run ten miles,
ridden a stationary bike and an elliptical, and lifted
weights, usually before the sun comes up.

Somewhere along the line, my dad's routine must
have affected me, because last year, even though I'm not
a runner, I decided to run a marathon and to ask my dad to run
it with me. When I called to talk with him about it, my dad's
first response was yes, followed immediately by, "But aren't you
going to Africa next week? Where do you think you will train?"

The next week I went to Zambia to work with my friend Chris,
teaching coaches how to share the love of Jesus through soccer.

I planned to stay in Zambia for two months, and in light of the conversation I had with my dad, I decided I'd better start running. As Chris and I were driving from the airport to my guesthouse, I said, "Hey, Chris, I see there are a lot of people walking around on the street, but does anyone here like to run?"

"Of course!" Chris said. "Zambians love to run, but usually it's when they are chasing after a ball."

"Well, what about on the street?" I said.

"Why would people play soccer on the street?" he replied. Chris seemed to be confused.

"I'm not talking about playing soccer. I want to know if people ever run for exercise, on the street."

Chris laughed. "The only time I see people running on the street in Lusaka is if they are trying to catch a taxi!"

As we arrived at the guesthouse, and Chris dropped me off, I started to think, *Running in Zambia might not be as easy as I thought.*

I went for my first run through the streets of Lusaka, the capital of Zambia, the next day. It didn't take long to realize that Chris was right; people weren't accustomed to seeing someone run down the street for fun. While I was met with plenty of awkward glances, cars honking, and several people yelling at me as I passed by, running on those particular roads was made even more difficult because there were no sidewalks, and for the most part the streets were just unpaved mounds of undulating rock and dirt.

As I was running, I jumped over numerous potholes and escaped a pack of wild dogs that decided to chase after me. I even dodged an oncoming semitruck. I didn't run very far, and when I returned to my room, I seriously considered calling my dad right then to inform him that we needed to postpone our race.

But then I thought, *I can't give up after just one attempt. I'll go out tomorrow and try one more time to run on the street.*

Over the next few weeks I ran around the immediate neighborhood where I was staying, dodging cars, busses, people, and animals of all types. As I ran, I kept thinking, *This is hard. This is difficult. This is a horrible place to run.* It never became any easier.

I tried my best to stay positive. I tried to psych myself up each day before my run, but inevitably I'd leave my guesthouse and begin to head down the dusty streets, and I'd think, *This was a very bad decision; running in Africa really isn't for me.*

After a few weeks most people became accustomed to seeing the strange white man running by. As I passed them, some people would just look and some would point; sometimes they would laugh. But I'd just smile, give a little wave, and say, "*Muli shani,*" which means "Hello" in Bemba, the local language, and then I'd continue on my way.

One day as I was running I passed a small house made of mud and thatch. In front of the house sat a woman on a small stool, washing laundry in a bright orange plastic bucket. She whistled as she scrubbed the clothes. There were also several little kids; I didn't count, but I'd guess there were at least ten of them playing in the yard. All seemed to be between eight and twelve years old.

As I approached the house, I noticed that none of the kids had any socks or shoes, or shirts, and some weren't even wearing pants. But regardless, they all bounced around the yard, singing, dancing, smiling, and laughing as they kicked a bunch of trash they had formed into a ball.

The kids didn't notice me until I had almost passed their house, but when they did, one little boy pointed and then screamed in fear, "*Mazungu!*" which means "white man" in most of Africa. All the kids immediately ran into the house.

Intrigued by the kids' response toward me, I decided to run the same route the next day. I was met by the exact same response; the kids saw me coming, started screaming "*Mazungu, mazungu!*" and then all ran inside the house.

As the days passed and I continued to run by that house, the kids were always playing in the yard. I would always smile and wave and the kids would always run and hide. But one day, as I was preparing to run by the house, I noticed something new. The kids were all there, playing in the yard without any socks or shoes, but when they saw me coming down the road that day they didn't run and hide; instead they froze like statues and pretended they couldn't see me.

I ran past that house and those kids playing in the yard almost every day for a month, and every single time the kids would see me they would all stop in their tracks and stand perfectly still until I had passed. I tried different tactics in an attempt to engage the kids in a conversation. I dribbled a ball. I threw candy. I even dressed like a ninja and pretended to karate chop their feet. But still, every day, the kids would pretend to be statues, acting like they were stone figures unable to see me or move.

But one day, completely out of the blue, one little boy, who had been frozen in his normal stance, smiled and then waved as I passed; he even did a little dance. The next day that same little boy did the exact same thing, but just as I was passing by he started to run with me. The first day he just ran until we were a few houses down. The next day he ran a few houses more. By the third day, most of the little boys and girls joined him, about ten in all, and we ran together around the entire block.

I had gone to Zambia to teach coaches to share the love of Jesus through soccer. I hadn't planned to befriend those kids, to run with them, or to share about how Jesus offers an outrageous life to anyone who connects their life to his. But over the two months I spent in Zambia, that's exactly what I did. And as I was running down the street each day, sometimes complaining about the difficulty of the terrain, God was there all along, directing, steering, and guiding my steps according to his outrageous plan for me.

I've noticed that the outrageous life isn't always the path of least resistance, but like any journey, it's filled with ups and downs. The thing is, when you journey with Jesus as your guide, no matter where you happen to be, or wherever you may go, God will use every opportunity along the way to make his glory known.

CONCLUSION

It All Begins with a Simple Prayer

A FEW YEARS AGO I was hanging out with some kids on the side of a freeway—it was the only grass they could find to play on in their neighborhood. These kids didn't have much, but they had an old, beat-up soccer ball they were using to play their game. After watching them play for a while, I walked up to the kid who appeared to be the leader, held out my brand-new soccer ball, and said, "Hey, do you want to make a trade?" All the kids laughed. They thought I was joking. So I said again, "I want to trade my ball for yours."

Though the kids couldn't understand why I would trade a brand-new, unused soccer ball for their beat-up, worn-out ball, I eventually convinced them I was serious. I wanted the kids' ball for two reasons. First, I wanted *them* to have a new ball to play with because of the joy I knew it would bring them. I figured a trade was only fair. But I also wanted their ball as a reminder of why I was there. The kids' ball was old and clearly well used.

That's what I want for my life: I want to be well used. I don't want to come to the end of my life and wonder what might have, could have, or should have been. I'm willing to be a little beat-up if it means that God is able to use me and everything he's given me for the purpose for which it was given.

———

Jesus chose twelve people to become his closest friends, and ultimately to carry the hope of his life, death, and resurrection to the world. The twelve people he chose weren't necessarily the most gifted, talented, good-looking, or intelligent. In fact, outsiders described them as unschooled, ordinary men, but when they placed their faith in Jesus and opened themselves to something more than their ordinary experience, outrageous things began to happen. Two thousand years later, I think God still offers ordinary people the opportunity to live in unconventional, extravagant, and remarkable ways. Jesus offers anyone who would place their faith in him a life that surpasses all reasonable bounds.

I know it seems crazy that God would choose to use ordinary people to accomplish his extraordinary purposes in the world, but he does. The question is, *are you awake to the unexpected opportunities, events, and adventure God makes available to* you?

Just like you, I'm on a journey, daily learning what it means to be awake to the life God wants for me. I no longer aspire to a passive state of existence. I'm unwilling to simply surrender myself to the rhythm of routine or to accept the cycle of monotony that can easily envelop our lives. I want to experience the life Jesus came to offer, but it doesn't just happen. It begins with a willingness to depart from the ordinary and a decision to be alert, attentive, and ready to embrace outrageous opportunities, events, and adventures amid our everyday life.

You might not ever move houses, change jobs, or travel the world, but you can still experience the outrageous life God has to offer. I think the most important step is to decide. God does the rest.

I don't think there's a complicated formula to experience the outrageous life. For me, it began with a simple prayer:

God, I invite you to do outrageous things through me.

I've been praying that simple prayer every day for almost twenty years now. I've realized that if you are willing, God is able. It's just that simple. So, go—be outrageous. What do you have to lose?

ACKNOWLEDGMENTS

I HAVE SPENT MOST OF MY LIFE ON A TEAM, and this book is the product of a team effort! In fact, most of the stories in this book are rooted in community and would not have been possible without a countless crew of extraordinary individuals whom I feel blessed to call coconspirators and friends. A few of your names appear in these stories, but most of you are unnamed heroes who have faithfully revealed Jesus to me in tangible ways through the outrageous adventures we've participated in together.

It took me thirty-four years, eleven months, and three hundred and forty-four days to locate the woman I always believed God had for me. Ginny—you are a truly extraordinary woman who daily reminds me that God has good plans for his children, far better than I could have ever hoped or imagined. It's a joy and honor for me to be on this life adventure with *you*!

Many people thank their literary agent in this section of a book, and I have often wondered if it's an obligatory notation or something more genuine. Trust me when I say, Tawny Johnson and D. C. Jacobson, that this book would still be a collection of experiences exclusively shared with close friends around the dinner table if it hadn't been for your encouragement, support, belief, and yes, even your brutal honesty at times. Tawny—I can't thank you enough for helping me to develop these stories into something that could become more widely accessible. You are a coconspirator, a blessing, and a friend!

When I was thirteen years old, my parents allowed me to travel to Europe—*alone*. I stopped in Detroit, Michigan, took a taxi from the airport, and found my hotel. I ate dinner at a restaurant called Bob's Big Boy. I took a taxi back to the airport the next day and flew to Amsterdam by myself. Mom and Dad, that might have been your best plan to get rid of me, but I'm certain it had more to do with your desire for me to learn that God is with us no matter where we go—even in Detroit. Thank you for how you have always encouraged me to dream and, even more, to take action on the dream I have. I am who I am today through your love, guidance, influence, and support.

Pete and Toni Donoghue—I'm like the relative you never asked for, never wanted, and can't get rid of, but after six years of living in the same house, you're stuck with me. I wish my words could sufficiently express my gratitude for your investment in my life, and saying thank you is simply not enough. You have had a profound and lasting impact on me, but *thank you* will have to do for now.

Andrea and Wesley—you have come a long way from the days spent fighting over Easter baskets and fake tattoos. I won't lie, I was a bit worried in the early days, but you have both become amazing young women who love God and are now living your own life adventure. Andrea, thank you for all your advice on this book, and also your chocolate chip cookies when needed.

To my friends at Ambassadors Football—it is a privilege to serve God with you. Jon Ortlip—thank you for serving as a pioneer in the work and mobilizing a group of ordinary soccer players to join God in what he had prepared in advance to do through soccer in every corner of the world. Your friendship and example of how to humbly seek God is invaluable.

Mike Moore and Jim Todd—almost twenty years ago you leveraged your influence and stood in the gap on my behalf. The impact of your support and encouragement might never fully be known this side of heaven, but let me just say, it's *big*. You are both heroes of the faith to me. Thank you so much for believing that our God could take an ordinary kid from Manteca and do extraordinary things. Because you believed that for me and countless others, the world will never be the same!

Rebekah Guzman—*thank you* for seeing the potential of this project when very few others could. I so appreciate your vision, perspective, and commitment to communicating transformational messages with the next generations. I look forward to many more opportunities to work together in the future!

Liz Heaney—for many months you were my favorite and absolutely *least* favorite person, all at the same time. Thank you for your patience and assistance helping a soccer-guy craft a message that could have broad appeal. It feels like I attended a master class in writing. I am privileged to have sat under your instruction.

Matt Clark—you are a dreamer, confidant, and friend. Your encouragement has pushed me to do things I would have probably stopped pursuing had it not been for you. I'm not sure if I should be angry or rejoice; only time will tell. I can't wait to see what God has for us just around the corner. You are a great example to many, my friend.

David Dwyer—you the man! I can't imagine the past six years absent of our Skyping, dreaming, and conspiring together for God's fame. Gates might have been a good boss, but I guarantee you traded up!

Alan Walker—the streets are hot. That's probably enough recognition, but I'll just add that you are truly gifted of God, and I believe your thoughts will ultimately shape generations to come. Without your creative insight and conceptual consultation, this book would look very different—in almost every way!

Lud Gold—you are a rock. Your friendship, mentorship, advice, and example have been a beacon of light in an often-clouded world.

Stephen Burks and Good City Productions—you are ultra-talented, creative, and uniquely positioned. Thank you for the ways you selflessly seek to partner with me. I appreciate you.

Aaron DeLoach—thank you for your support and encouragement. It was fun working together on this project. It will be more fun working together on *your* book—the best is still to come.

Wayne Walker—thank you for the countless hours spent listening to these stories and the encouragement you are to me. I'm praying about becoming your full-time caddy. I'm also praying that your introduction comes to pass.

Finally, I want to thank you, reader. My greatest passion is to participate in the outrageous adventure found in everyday faith. My next greatest passion is to talk about those adventures with you. Thank you for allowing me to come into your life and share a small picture of what God continues to teach me about the outrageous life of faith. I believe there is power in stories—I'd love to hear yours as well.

Aaron Tredway is the vice president of global advancement for Ambassadors Football, a nonprofit organization that works for the transformation of individuals and communities through indigenous football outreach. Raised in California, Aaron has spent the last eighteen years of his life playing and coaching professional soccer on six continents.

With two degrees in physical education and two degrees in theology (including a doctorate of ministry from Liberty University), Aaron was one of the founders and executive director of the US-based professional soccer team Cleveland City Stars, and has a passion to inspire and mentor professional athletes. Aaron and his wife, Ginny, currently reside in Cleveland with their son, Noah, where Aaron serves as teaching pastor of Fellowship Bible Church.

CONNECT WITH AARON

VISIT
AARONTREDWAY.COM
AND
AMBASSADORSFOOTBALL.ORG

Outrageous adventures in friendship!

AN ORIGINAL SERIES AT
WWW.BIGWORLDLITTLEBALL.COM

Join Aaron Tredway and Dana McGregor, two best friends who have traveled the world together for the last twenty years playing professional soccer and having hilarious and outrageous adventures. From the jungles of Africa to the world's largest cities including Mumbai, Bangalore, and Las Vegas, Aaron and Dana always manage to connect with people through soccer. Nothing is scripted. Nothing is contrived. When Dana and Aaron are together, anything can happen — and it usually does!

Connect with

Relevant. Intelligent. Engaging.

Sign up for announcements about
new and upcoming titles at

www.bakerbooks.com/signup

 ReadBakerBooks

 ReadBakerBooks